CANCELED LIVES

Also by Blake Bailey

Philip Roth: The Biography

The Splendid Things We Planned: A Family Portrait

Farther & Wilder: The Lost Weekends and Literary Dreams of Charles Jackson

Cheever: A Life

A Tragic Honesty: The Life and Work of Richard Yates

CANCELED LIVES

My Father, My Scandal, and Me

BLAKE BAILEY

Skyhorse Publishing

Skyhorse Publishing books may be purchased in bulk at special discounts for sales promotion, corporate gifts, fund-raising, or educational purposes. Special editions can also be created to specifications. For details, contact the Special Sales Department, Skyhorse Publishing, 307 West 36th Street, 11th Floor, New York, NY 10018 or info@skyhorsepublishing.com.

Skyhorse® and Skyhorse Publishing® are registered trademarks of Skyhorse Publishing, Inc.®, a Delaware corporation.

Visit our website at www.skyhorsepublishing.com.

Please follow our publisher Tony Lyons on Instagram @tonylyonsisuncertain

10 9 8 7 6 5 4 3 2 1

Library of Congress Cataloging-in-Publication Data is available on file.

Cover design by David Ter-Avanesyan
Cover images courtesy of Blake Bailey and Getty Images

Print ISBN: 978-1-5107-8331-7
Ebook ISBN: 978-1-5107-8332-4

Printed in the United States of America

Contents

"By nature, I am not an introspective person."
—From a rather introspective letter my father wrote
me on April 12, 2014

". . . count no man happy until he dies, free of pain
at last."
—Sophocles, *Oedipus Rex*

To Burck

Chapter One

SWEETHEART

When my phone pinged early Sunday morning, November 14, 2021, I knew it was because my father, Burck, was either dead or about to die. Like Mike Campbell's bankruptcy in *The Sun Also Rises,* this had come on gradually and then suddenly. Three months earlier, our long-fractured family had gathered in Santa Fe for my father's eighty-seventh birthday. I hadn't seen my two stepsiblings, Kelli and Aaron, in seventeen years; ditto their mother, Sandra, whose speech had been reduced to a sad, strangulated baying by a stroke. Still, everyone was on their best behavior, and my father seemed in decent fettle. He wheezed a bit while walking uphill with his COVID mask on, but was otherwise spry enough to make breakfast for me and my seventeen-year-old daughter, visit museums, and show us around the Plaza during Indian Market weekend.

The wheezing and wet cough worsened, however, and a month later he got a chest X-ray followed by a CT scan. With studied understatement, he noted that the radiology report didn't "seem too good"—and no, it didn't:

> Impression: There is a large necrotic mass in the left lower lobe most worrisome for primary lung cancer. There is broad pleural contact laterally with associated pleural effusion. There are metastatic lymph nodes at the left hilum and subcarinal region. These nodes are mildly enlarged with a component of central necrosis.

"Not sure where I go from here," Burck concluded, "but I guess I'll hear from the doctor's office in due course."

My own life had been destroyed by scandal a few months before, and I was back living in my hometown—Oklahoma City, sigh—for the first time in thirty-odd years. A lifelong friend and bonafide saint, Dr. Matt, had invited me to stay in his small but nice garage apartment, overlooking a pool and tennis court. Matt was fond of both my parents (his own parents were my godparents), and I summoned him to discuss Burck's radiology report. He urged me to look on the bright side: if it were, in fact, lung cancer, they could still theoretically remove the affected lymph nodes and treat other areas with radiation. I shared this with my father.

I went on emailing him almost every morning between that dire radiology report on October 5 and that ominous early-morning text-ping on November 14. His replies tended to be on the laconic side—a few sentences mustered amid a vertiginous exhaustion. I kept offering to visit him in Santa Fe and help in whatever way I could, but he kept me at a long arm's length. He didn't feel like having visitors at the moment, he said, but meanwhile my stepsister—who'd always elicited a kind of tender deference from Burck that I couldn't help envying—was another matter. She had her own pied-à-terre in Santa Fe and came and went chez Burck as she pleased, taking him to doctor appointments (three inconclusive biopsies) and the like. At one point she told me that Burck was staying alive, barely, for my stepmother's sake.

Around this time I slept poorly and woke every morning with a kind of panicky, sympathetic malaise, as if I were dying right along with my father. Of course the malaise had other sources too; my life was relatively fucked whether Burck went on living or not, but I didn't need it to be any *more* fucked. In any case, I knew what to make of that plangent text-ping on November 14, 2021: "Blake it's Aaron," my stepbrother had written. "You need to call me asap." Sure enough, my father was dying.

I proposed to drive immediately to Santa Fe, about ten hours, and called my stepsister to let her know I was coming. For her part she explained that she'd found Burck slumped against a wall that morning, overtaken by exhaustion en route to the toilet. In a kind of wondering way he'd announced that he was dying today, and what a nice day to do it (nodding toward a sun-brightened window). When I called, he was back in bed but still conscious, so she put him on the phone. I said I was heading out the door and would see him soon.

"I think I'll still be here," he said in a slow, gluey voice.

"I certainly hope so, sweetheart."

I'd never called my formidable father *sweetheart*, and would have chosen a manlier endearment if I'd been in my right mind. On the other hand it seemed oddly appropriate, and, after all, this was a man I'd called Papa and kissed on the lips all my life, even at the worst of times, or some of them anyway.

Chapter Two

CHRONICLE OF A DEATH FORETOLD

A mere seven months before, I was the happiest I'd ever been: husband to a woman I loved and admired (despite strains in our marriage that were entirely my fault), father of a delightful sixteen-year-old daughter, and author of a nine-hundred-page literary biography that was dominating book-chat pages and would presently lead to my ruin. But let me relive the nice part first—my little cock crow (or what one commentator described as my "all-too-evident pride, bordering on hubris") just before the bomb exploded and the radioactive half-life set in.

And it happened just like that: a flash, and it was over. The peak of my success and the nadir of my fall overlapped within days or hours. *Philip Roth: The Biography* was published on April 6, 2021, when I was already aware of the forthcoming front-page rave by Cynthia Ozick (!) for the April 11 *New York Times Book Review*: "The 19th-century novel lives on. Its name today is Biography; its nature is that of Dostoyevskian magnitude. And Blake Bailey's comprehensive life of Philip Roth—to tell it outright—is a narrative masterwork." Suffice it to say, I never expected Cynthia Ozick to notice my existence, much less in the context of Dostoyevskian magnitude. With her help, though—not to say that of Roth's legion of detractors (soon to become mine)—I enjoyed a week or two of cultural ubiquity, at least by the standards of literary biography. For a slick, seven-minute segment on *CBS Saturday Morning*, Jeff Glor (who reminded me pleasantly, in person, of William Hurt in *Broadcast News*) called my book "towering . . . one of the most anticipated biographies in years"; Joe and Mika, Christiane Amanpour, Anthony Scaramucci yet, chatted with me about Roth, cancel culture, and the like; I was the subject of a mostly sympathetic *New York Times Magazine* profile; best of all, perhaps, I'd been asked to deliver that year's Leon Levy Biography Lecture, whose past luminaries included Hermione Lee, Richard Holmes, Ron Chernow, and Robert Caro . . . Caro! Caro and me, me and Caro—it scarcely computes. Finally, at the end of that first week of publication (while Enola Gay's shadow edged closer and closer), I debuted at number twelve on the *New York Times* bestseller list—the only nine-hundred-page lit bio on the list, I hope needless to say.

But there were ominous forces afoot. "Just wondering," Josh Glancy of the London *Times* emailed me, almost three weeks before publication, "whether you're concerned at all about Roth getting 'canceled'? It seems like there's hunger out there to savage him, in some quarters." I wrote a rather startled, demurring reply, but sure enough Glancy's piece quoted a number of female academics who seemed incensed about things—all the more now that they'd been made aware of certain revelations in my book. The *Daily Mail* noted Roth's "misogyny and sexual depravity" in an unsubtle headline that likewise bruited the possibility he'd be "CANCELED." In the latter case, especially, I wondered if the reporter was remotely aware of Roth's cultural importance, aside from the usual epithet "Pulitzer Prize–winning author"; my book had certainly highlighted aspects of Roth's wayward nature, though I wasn't inclined to label him an actual misogynist (much less a depraved one), or to label him period. And yet my book was the immediate cause of the uproar.

Oddly enough, a couple of the most prominent early reviews (invariably described as "prescient" once my own degeneracy had been revealed) hammered the point that I was not only sympathetic but "complicitous" with Roth—"exceptionally attuned to his grievances," said Laura Marsh in the *New Republic*, describing me as Roth's "adoring wingman" vis-à-vis the women in his life; my book, said Parul Sehgal in the daily *New York Times*, was "a sprawling apologia for Roth's treatment of women, on and off the page, and a minutely detailed account of his victimization at the hands of his two wives." Hard words, and I wondered: How did my allegedly strenuous efforts to whitewash Roth's behavior toward women—as Marsh and Sehgal and various others (especially later) would have it—square with the movement to cancel Roth *because* of the "misogyny and sexual depravity" which had been exposed *in my book* . . . ? Marsh's attempt to reconcile this paradox struck me as a little tortured: Despite my utter failure to challenge Roth's "moral accounting," she wrote, ". . . the result is not a final winning of the argument, as Roth might have hoped. . . . this sympathetic biography makes him a spiteful obsessive." But wait: either I meant to be sympathetic or I meant to make him a spiteful obsessive; can it be both? Or maybe what I mainly meant was to be nuanced and objective.

I was still smarting from these lashes when I learned that Pamela Paul, the *New York Times* book editor, wanted to interview me for her podcast. This was a day or two after Sehgal had pilloried me in the daily *Times*, and a day or two *before* Ozick's front-page rave in the Sunday *Times* would make its first appearance online. Meanwhile I didn't know what the hell to expect from the latter, but I was pretty sure one wasn't featured on the podcast if one's book was about to be panned outright, so I figured it had to be a good augury. Still, I took special pains to be mild and engaging with the formidable Paul—my "pride, bordering on hubris" well in check—and only my final remarks smack a little of protesting too much:

> **BB:** There's been a lot of talk about Philip as a misogynist, and canceling him, and so forth. And kind of the worst part of this task is you can't make everybody happy with a biography of Philip Roth. They either love him or they hate him, and the people who love him think you're too hard on him, and the people

who hate him think you're not hard enough. Philip brought a lot of this on himself; he could behave very badly, and if you took exception to that, he would mock you [laugh] for doing so. . . . But I want people to bear in mind that he was an extremely complicated human being, and part of Philip was a darling, darling man. There is a reason that six or seven or eight of his former lovers came to visit him at his bedside when he was dying. And I *saw* that; I was *there*. . . . So you must be doing something right if you have that many people who love you so dearly.

PP: Well, I hope you're wrong about readers—that there aren't just people who love or hate him, but that there are people in between. Because, as you say, he was complicated, most people are complicated, so hopefully people have more nuanced and complicated and open opinions or are open to hearing more about Philip Roth.

BB: I hope so, too.

The podcast aired on April 9, the Ozick review appeared gorgeously in print two days later, and I was permitted a week or so of relative happiness. Then *boom* . . . and there I was, as smoldering and bewildered as Wile E. Coyote after his latest Acme contraption has backfired. All my media events were canceled one after the other: I'd already had Zoom chats with interlocutors such as Peter Sagal, Don Winslow, Alexandra Schwartz, and Mary Karr, but the ones to come (e.g., with Francine Prose, who took to saying hard things about me, as did Schwartz and Karr) were off, ditto my talks at the 92Y, Edith Wharton's home in Lenox, Massachusetts, the Philip Roth Reading Room at the Newark Public Library . . . I knew it was only a matter of time (days, hours) before Kai Bird, the head of the Levy Center for Biography and a very decent man, found the words to excuse me from their annual lecture, and I spared him the trouble with a sorrowful email that he received with seemly regret.

Weeks or centuries later I was back in my home state of Oklahoma: my twenty-one-year marriage was over, and my wife and daughter were a thousand miles away; Google News Alert (which I would have canceled except that I needed to keep my lawyer posted about the more alarming developments) reminded me of my worsening pariah status every day or two, and yet I was far away from the noise on the Eastern Seaboard and that, at least, was faint comfort. One night I had dinner with a well-heeled friend (at his house, lest he be seen in public with me), and he handed over a recent *New York* magazine, where I appeared in the Highbrow/Despicable quadrant of its Approval Matrix: "Roth bio put on hold* after **horrific** Blake Bailey allegations emerge." I wondered, not without a kind of curious gratification, whether I was the only person ever to be dubbed Highbrow/Despicable *and* Highbrow/Brilliant, at any rate within weeks of each other.

And that's pretty much how I console myself these days: I'm a complicated person, just like Philip Roth, or you, and I can't be reduced to a label such as rapist, groomer, or what

---

* And subsequently canceled by W. W. Norton & Company. See Appendix.

you will. (Another consolation: I'll never Google myself or go anywhere near Twitter/X again.) And I mean to be frank here—to *let the repellent in,* as Roth liked to say. This is your trigger warning.

Chapter Three

TWO AND A HALF INCHES

Toward the end of the movie *Five Easy Pieces*, a bitter young man played by Jack Nicholson pushes his wheel-chair-bound father into an open field and then crouches to have a talk with him. The father, struck dumb by a stroke, stares impassively while Jack does his best to explain his wayward life: "I'm trying to imagine your half of this conversation. My feeling is, I don't know, that if you could talk we wouldn't be talking. . . . You all right? I don't know what to say—" Here he begins to cry, and so do I (even now, just thinking about it). The father's fixed expression is one of vast pitying hopelessness. "The best I can do is apologize," Jack says at last, "and we both know I was never really that good at it anyway."

I'm also haunted by a scene from Edmund Gosse's *Father and Son*: the eight-year-old Edmund has just lost his mother to breast cancer, and he and his righteous but loving father comfort each other in total silence as night falls and the room turns dark. Alone in the world except for each other.

HERE'S THE OPENING of my father's obituary, which appeared in various newspapers and the *Oklahoma Bar Journal*:

> Burck Bailey was born on August 22, 1934, in Vinita, Oklahoma, to Frank and Frances (Burckhalter) Bailey, and died on November 18, 2021, at the age of 87. Upon graduation in 1952 from Vinita High School, where he was voted the outstanding member of the Senior class, Burck was awarded the Oklahoma Honor Scholarship by Westminster College in Fulton, Missouri. After two years of Westminster, he volunteered to serve in the U. S. Army to qualify for the G. I. Bill to help finance his education. After completing two years of Army service stationed near Stuttgart, Germany, Burck returned to Westminster, . . . [where he] served as President of his fraternity and various other campus organizations, and graduated with Honors in 1958.
>
> Burck was one of twenty men in the United States who received a Root-Tilden Scholarship to New York University School of Law, from which he graduated in 1961 . . .

Outstanding member of his senior class! Bootstrapped his way through college via an Honor Scholarship and the

G. I. Bill! President of his fraternity (Phi Delta Theta)! One of twenty nationwide Root-Tilden Scholars at NYU Law! The kind of "fifties golden boy" embodied by the titular hero of Calvin Trillin's *Remembering Denny:* a legendary Yalie who, however, lost his way and went on to lead a life of grinding disappointment—"a man who didn't know who he was," my father opined, inscribing the book to me. Presumably, when you knew who you were, and had the right values, your golden-boy life "had the smooth trajectory of an airliner rising from the ground," as Trillin wrote—and so, it seems, with my father:

> . . . [Burck's] distinguished career included service as President of the Oklahoma Bar Association in 1988. He previously served as President of the Oklahoma County Bar Association in 1983-1984. He received the Oklahoma Bar Association Professionalism Award in 1989. The citation read in part, "His conduct, honesty, integrity, and courtesy best exemplify and represent the highest standards of the legal profession." . . .
>
> Burck's forensic skills extended beyond the trial courtroom and included extensive appellate practice. He presented oral arguments in State and Federal appellate courts around the country, including three appearances before the United States Supreme Court . . .

A few people asked me whether *I* wrote the obit, since I'm a writer (or was in my former life) and the obit is well-written enough and comprehensive to the point of fulsomeness. A proper act of filial homage. Sorry to say, though, I didn't know my father's career in nearly such granular detail—*outstanding member of his senior class?*—nor did I know, say, that one makes a distinction between trial and appellate practice, etc. In fact, the author and the subject are one and the same. Composing this panegyric was how my father spent his last lucid days on earth, which I suppose is one reason he didn't want to be distracted by visits from his only (surviving) biological son.

His self-authored obit notwithstanding, Burck had a well-earned reputation for humility. "Oh, my, I'm embarrassed now," he mutters during a videotaped interview (mailed to me after a long estrangement), when his off-screen interlocutor, Judge Ralph Thompson, refers to him as "the preeminent trial lawyer" in the long history of the Western District of Oklahoma. Of course Burck took pride in his own accomplishments, but he also knew that people would be more inclined to praise him if he didn't go out of his way to praise himself. Also he was truly, if paradoxically, a modest man: one of the reasons he worked so damnably hard, all his life, was because he always suspected he wasn't smart enough.

Was it this nagging sense of inadequacy that made him, sometimes, less than generous vis-à-vis the little achievements of others, especially loved ones? My first substantial published book, a biography of the novelist Richard Yates, was published on my fortieth birthday—July 1, 2003—after I'd foundered as a would-be writer for almost twenty years. When I presented it to Burck, he turned it over in his hands (cocking his brow at that Vonnegut blurb), then said, showing me the book's spine: "Your two and a half inches of posterity." I've often longed to revisit that moment so I could tell him to shove the whole 671-page opus right up his ass.

And that was nothing next to our exchange two weeks later, when the *New York Times* declared my book to be "great, perceptive, heartbreaking . . . a landmark event." I lived near Gainesville, Florida, where my wife was a grad student, and I couldn't wait to phone Burck at his office in Oklahoma City. Our conversation went something like this:

> **ME:** Have you seen today's *New York Times*?
> **BURCK** (in a quietly irritable voice—a busy man distracted by trifles): Why do you ask?
> **ME:** Well, there's a review of my book . . .
> **BURCK:** Is it a bad review?
> **ME** (after a startled pause): No. Why—?
> **BURCK:** The *Harper's* review wasn't so good.

(In his *Harper's* roundup, John Leonard had given a brief paragraph to my book, deploring the folly of romanticizing a drunken fucking mess like Richard Yates.)

> **ME:** That wasn't really a considered review so much as a pious, pompous—
> **BURCK:** Ah! So you dismiss *that* review just because he said things you don't—
> **ME:** OK, OK . . . look. Why don't you just go to the newsstand and buy a copy of today's *Times*?
> **BURCK:** Well, I may or may not, son. Got a lot to do today.

I sometimes wonder whether I exaggerate my father's meanness on that occasion. After all, he could be so nice at other
times. God only knows what would have become of me
(wait: what *did* become of me?) without his help, financial
and otherwise, time and again. And it wasn't just me: "I
always knew I could call on him in a crisis," said his kindly
sister, Kay, "but I'm trying to think if he ever, once, gave
me a compliment of any size, big or small." My own definite
impression was that Burck found me a lot easier to take
when I was a failure.

Chapter Four

CLOWNISH LUSTS

Shortly after finishing my third and least ambitious literary biography—that *jeu d'esprit* about Charlie Jackson, author of *The Lost Weekend*—I mentioned to my wife that I was thinking about tackling "our greatest living novelist." My wife affected puzzlement: "You want to write a biography of Toni Morrison?"

Several years before, when I first proposed to try my hand at literary biography (having repeatedly failed as a fiction writer) with a book about Richard Yates, my wife was encouraging but a little bemused: I think she found Yates's work abysmally depressing and ditto his life (much of it passed in bars and madhouses, whenever he'd made the mistake of leaving his L-shaped desk). By the time I presented her with the freshly printed manuscript, however, she'd been a daily witness to my obsessive fourteen-month labor and was more than ready to like the book and its subject—reading the whole cinderblock almost in a single sitting and returning from our upstairs bedroom with tears in her eyes.

Between that high point and her reading of *Cheever*, six years later, fell the discovery of my infidelities (especially between the years 2003 and 2005), and hence she was all the more galled by Cheever's own delinquencies in that respect. At any rate her eyes were bone dry when she lucidly reported that a single paragraph had struck her as notably awkward (where I tried to describe the horrified reaction of a would-be paramour to Cheever's first sexual overture); she suggested a way to fix it, and I followed her advice pretty much to the letter. As for my Jackson book, well, by then she expected good work or at least competence, and assured me in a detached way that the manuscript was good to go.

By the time she read a draft of my Roth biography, our marriage remained on life support pretty much for the sole sake of our daughter, though we tried to be tender or at least civil to each other. I was on a solo road trip while our daughter was away at camp (more about that later) when my wife phoned to let me know her thoughts. First she congratulated me: with laudable objectivity, given my most problematic subject (not least in her eyes), she was bound to admit that my Roth book was perhaps, in a formal way, my best yet. However, there were things in it that readers (especially female) would find repugnant, and in those cases I had to make my disapproval a little more explicit. She was especially appalled by the way Roth, while teaching at

Penn in the seventies, had relied on his friend and colleague Joel Conarroe to play (as Joel put it) "the role of, pardon the expression, pimp"—i.e., by choosing women for Roth's over-subscribed class on the bases of looks and apparent susceptibility. In this and other respects, my wife foresaw more vividly than I what lay ahead if I didn't take a harder line against Roth's lapses, or, for that matter, even if I did. As always I took her advice up to a point, and badgered her afterward to help me with other bits my editor had found in need of tweaking.

Later, when our lives blew up, my wife let me know that this had been a bitter labor indeed, since her malaise toward the project had only waxed over time. It had been different with my three previous biographies. As I think they themselves would attest, the children and wives of my other (safely dead) subjects had enjoyed collaborating with me, and part of their good opinion was their good opinion of my wife. Cheever's eighty-six-year-old widow, Mary—who'd somehow endured forty-plus years with a prickly, alcoholic, sexually wayward husband—had met my eight-months-pregnant wife for the first time on a Westchester train platform; I seem to recall the widow placing a candid hand on my wife's stomach and chiding me, right off the bat, to take better care of both mother and child, as if she already suspected that I (like her dead husband) was delinquent somehow, or at least unworthy of the paragon she'd immediately deemed my wife to be. My main friendship among the Yates family was with the middle daughter and executor, Monica, who was capable of breathtaking candor if she found you (as I think she rarely did) deserving of her confidence. DreamWorks had flown my wife and me to the *Revolutionary Road* premiere in Los Angeles, and we were sitting by ourselves at the after-party—mulling our unsatisfactory meeting with the co-star, Leo DiCaprio, who'd wordlessly deserted us to rejoin his entourage—when Monica spotted us in the crowd and dropped beside us, confiding with a sigh that the movie wasn't *nearly* as good as she'd claimed in her little pre-screening speech. Thus I knew she'd sized up my wife and found her a good egg. And finally there was my wife's (and eleven-year-old daughter's) belated meeting with the genteel older daughter of Charles Jackson, Sarah, who'd come to the New School auditorium for the 2015 National Book Critics Circle finalists' reading (my memoir, *The Splendid Things We Planned,* was nominated) expressly to see me; after my wife and daughter had introduced themselves, then left us alone to chat, Sarah assured me in her shy way that I had a *lovely* family, as I certainly did.

In Roth's case, I worked with the living man for six years without ever broaching the possibility of his meeting my wife, who was all too familiar with certain passages in his work such as the one in *Portnoy* where the narrator vows never to enter into a contract to sleep with only one woman his entire life, no matter how many of his consorts threaten suicide in the meantime. For my part I can't deny that I shared Portnoy's (and Roth's) views about the hopelessness of monogamy to some extent, though I'd certainly *meant* to be faithful once I finally made the decision to settle down with so decent, intelligent, and loving a person as my wife, and shame on me for marrying at all if I couldn't keep that vow. My efforts were token at best: I was faithful for the first three years, and faithful again for almost five after May 2005, when my wife discovered, to her horror, my infidelity with a few former students once they were legal adults. Later I had two affairs (not concurrently) with married women who were well-known fellow writers.

Having one's "clownish lusts" (as Gabriel Conroy aptly reflects of himself in "The Dead") exposed in newspapers here and abroad is enough to put one off sex forever, and indeed a long time would pass before I was even able to kiss a person (other than family) after my disgrace. Writing about the subject is no picnic either. But *let the repellent in*, as Roth insisted: that was me, I did that, and it was disgustingly selfish and hurtful in some cases to all parties involved, especially my blameless wife. And yet: one may be inconstant without being a predator or a misogynist; indeed, one may be a doting parent and have other sterling qualities besides. I've always liked Maugham's comment, in *The Razor's Edge*, on the subject of poor Sophie's promiscuity: "That doesn't mean she's bad. Quite a number of highly respected citizens get drunk and have a liking for rough trade. They're bad habits, like biting one's nails, but I don't know that they're worse than that. I call a person bad who lies and cheats and is unkind."

I did a fair amount of lying and cheating (albeit only when it came to sex), so call me bad on those points. And if undoing the worst of it would bring back my once-happy life— and unhurt my wife and daughter—I wouldn't hesitate. But certainly I didn't foresee the day when such sins would be so grievously punished, and I can't help wondering whether

it would have been better if I were a professional basket-
ball player, or a heavy metal guitarist, or Rob Lowe—just
about anything not concerned with publishing, journalism,
or academia.

Chapter Five

LIKE FATHER
LIKE SON

My father and I were alike in many ways. For one thing
we had a basically cynical view of the world. "Don't
you want to be a Regular Guy?" Burck said to me, wryly,
when I was still a kid and therefore someone to dote on
(most of the time). With the "Regular Guy" comment Burck
was encouraging me, obliquely, to follow a less beaten path
in life, and so I would. "When I die," he also liked to say,
"stick a bone up my ass and let the dogs drag me away"—
which nicely reflected his rationalistic view of life; his old
catchphrase occurred to me when I found him dead and
stood gazing at his sad, depleted corpse. We also looked
and sounded alike (his sister remarked that she'd once
heard Burck on TV in another room and thought he was

me, or vice versa), and both of us had a great capacity for work when our self-esteem was at stake.

But there were crucial differences. Our kindred cynicism, for one, was deceptive: my father's was belied by a great, almost parodic earnestness about certain conventional values, which he embodied in every phase of his public life— and I'm impressed by this paradox (a word that comes up a lot in my musing about Burck): in this respect he abundantly satisfied F. Scott Fitzgerald's "test of a first-rate intelligence," to wit: "the ability to hold two opposing ideas in mind at the same time and still retain the ability to function. One should, for example, be able to see that things are hopeless yet be determined to make them otherwise."

And hence perhaps the biggest difference between Burck and me: He was born in a crap town (Vinita, OK) at the bottom of the Depression, from which he rose doggedly and quasi-humbly to his eminence as the Best Trial Lawyer the state ever produced; I was born amid the upper-middle-class comfort that he provided for me, and my relative purblind cockiness (perversely encouraged by a sardonic father) would eventually lead to my ruin. Also, Burck came of age in the fifties, when "moral glamor was the rage" (Philip Roth) among American men, when one was encouraged to value oneself according to the number of crushing burdens (marriage, children, career) one was willing to assume— whereas I, child of a more ironized ethos, tended to scoff at conventional morality or conventional anything. Burck's dual nature, in other words, made any comparison with his wiseass second-born problematic. No wonder my older brother, Scott—a failure by any yardstick—liked to refer to

Burck as the Wizard of Oz, i.e., the great infallible figure in public, and the mordant bumbler behind the curtain in private fact. Like most of my brother's pronouncements, this was both grossly unfair and percipient up to a point.

BURCK AND I also had a certain degree of lechery in common.

In 1958, he received one of the most lucrative/prestigious law scholarships in the country, the Root-Tilden at NYU, for which two of the best and brightest from each of the ten federal circuits were chosen yearly. Soon after, alas, the Burck jet was due to crash and smolder in the fields a while. According to his sister, Kay, he'd always had a thing for redheads—to be exact, redheads who resembled the actress Arlene Dahl, who was featured on the bedroom walls of his youth. By the time he graduated from Westminster, he was "pinned"—engaged to be engaged, basically—to a Dahl lookalike named Lydia, who attended Westminster's sister school, William Woods. The only story Burck ever told me about Lydia was the time he'd asked for his pin back and had to duck when she shied it at his head. Hitherto they'd been considered a power couple in the making: both smart, ambitious, personable, etc. The summer after Burck's first year at NYU, Lydia had come to Vinita (from Arkansas) chaperoned by her formidable mother, who advised Burck's sister not to be afraid of wearing a bit more makeup. Folks were impressed, and considered Lydia the perfect match for their golden boy. She was planning to visit him in New York that Christmas, when everyone expected Burck to pop the question.

But Burck was born restless and had seen the world by then, and now was frequenting jazz clubs in Greenwich Village. One day he spotted my twenty-year-old mother, Marlies (née Neumann), waiting for an elevator in Hayden Hall, the law dorm on Washington Square: "She was very trim and wearing pink pedal pushers," he remembered. "She had long hair and a nose too big for her (then) thin face, but I thought she was quite attractive in a quirky kind of way." The young Marlies looked something like young Shirley MacLaine, albeit with a longer nose and brown hair instead of red. She was fresh off the boat from Germany and making the most of her hard-won distance from burgherish parents. Probably she was at Hayden Hall that day to visit her friend Mickey Donner, whose room was on the same floor as Burck's and who was happy to arrange a blind date. Burck took the fetching German girl to an East Village club, where Mickey (whose father was a booking agent) had scored tickets for them to see the great jazz trombonist Jack Teagarden. Anyway the date was a hit, which boded ill for Burck's future otherwise.

Burck and I were estranged when my memoir *The Splendid Things We Planned* was published, in 2014, but once he got back in touch (because he'd read the memoir) he pointed out that he'd almost died of a bleeding ulcer *before*, not after, his marriage to Marlies, who was three months pregnant at the time, news of which was the immediate cause of Burck's ulcer. Also it was his roommate, Del McQuaide, *not* my mother (as I wrote in *Splendid*), who found Burck passed out in a pool of blood and saved his life by calling an ambulance in the nick of time. Afterward Marlies visited Burck at St. Vincent's, where they commiserated about their predicament and decided to get married.

So the ulcer not only led to an unhappy marriage and *very* tortured family life, but also permanently undermined my father's health. I noticed his weight was given as 170 on his Army Registration Certificate of 1954, or roughly twenty-five pounds more than he ever weighed during my lifetime, and almost fifty pounds more than he weighed in his final decade or so, when Marlies was fond of pointing out that her ex-husband looked "like a Buchenwald survivor." In brief: when his peptic ulcer had persisted throughout his twenties, Burck had gotten an antrectomy with vagotomy—removal of part of his stomach plus the vagus nerve controlling production of stomach acid—which resulted in a lifetime of chronic diarrhea, as many as ten to twelve loose stools a day in Burck's case, despite the two Imodium tablets he always took to avoid sprinting out of courtrooms with a redolent bulge in his pants.

For most of my life I was under the impression that Burck and Marlies had been less than candid about the circumstances of their marriage, though of course the Vinita rumor-mill had conjectured the worst, i.e., the truth. (One of my closest friends from childhood, Bentley Edmonds, also has Vinita roots—his mother is one of Aunt Kay's old school chums—and can attest that Burck's marriage was known among locals as the Scandal of Vinita.) Though they were married at Manhattan's First Presbyterian Church on May 28, 1960—photos show my mother already a size too big for her frumpy gray suit—they would usually give the date as the preceding January, or about ten months before my brother was born.

However, as I learned only recently, Burck could hardly have been more straightforward about things: after leaving St. Vincent's, he phoned his parents and manfully informed them that he'd knocked up a strange German girl and was naturally going to marry her. Instead of plotzing on the spot ("I go over there to kill the bastards," said Burck's father, a proud veteran of both world wars, "and he marries one!"), his parents made the best of things. "Miss Neumann, a graduate of Dusseldorf School of Languages," read the bewildered announcement in the *Vinita Daily Journal*, "is employed at the B. Altman department store in New York . . ." Burck's mother gave a soirée for her princeling son's then-blowzy bride—an occasion both Oma and her daughter would forever remember with ineffable horror: "Oh dear God," Kay told me, "I can't tell you what she looked like. . . . This *hair* sticking straight out like Annie Oakley, these pigtail things on either side of her head, with her short shorts and tee-shirt and probably no bra . . ." I think Marlies probably did wear a bra in 1960—though I don't think she even owned a bra during most of my childhood, after second-wave feminism hit—but the rest of the description is pretty spot-on. Once the Vinita hausfrauen had gathered, with their beauty-parlor do's and brand-clean finery, making with the usual chit-chat, Marlies stood it for maybe five minutes before ostentatiously dragging a chair within a foot or two of the TV and watching *Bonanza*.

And what of the red-haired Lydia? She would go on to be a high-ranking cabinet member in the Carter administration, and a lot of other impressive things besides, and many years later she and her would-be sister-in-law, Kay, met for lunch in Georgetown with a mutual friend. Lydia was pleasant as ever, and said not a word about Kay's older brother.

Chapter Six

GROOMING

Burck may have been a bit more lecherous than the average bear, but he was also uncommonly kind and generous to his fellow creatures—not least his second-born son, whom he subsidized well into adulthood. I was almost thirty when I decided I couldn't make a living as a writer (yet) and would need to find a steadier profession *asap*. In addition to the odd checks Burck had continued to send me out of the goodness of his heart, he agreed to give me $1,000 a month and pay my tuition for coursework leading to teacher certification, so I could dispense with the distraction of gainful employment. We'd originally agreed that I would pay him back in regular installments once I found a teaching job, and such was my earnestness that I got straight-As in my courses and swiftly landed what was arguably the best job in Orleans Parish: teacher of eighth-grade gifted students at one of the very few viable magnet schools. When I told Burck what my take-home pay was that first year, he refused to let me reimburse him, and seven years later he and his second wife, Sandra, and my nice Aunt Kay and her husband, Heidi, were all on hand when I was honored as Louisiana Humanities Teacher of the Year at the governor's mansion in Baton Rouge.

This happy memory was blighted twenty-one years later by allegations of my having "groomed" former students to have sex with me once they were no longer minors. That would suggest a certain amount of libidinous foresight on my part, though I remember thinking (to the extent I could think at all while my life was imploding) when I first encountered the term "grooming" on April 20, 2021, that it was a vast improvement over those first rumors, only a few days before, that I'd actually "assaulted" my students while they were in eighth-grade. (For what it's worth: I've taught middle-school students as young as eleven and graduate students as old as ninety-eight, and committed no carnal impropriety with any of them while they were still my students or legal minors.)

When the first stories about my depravity began to appear, I couldn't read them and still can't—it would be like injecting sulfuric acid into my heart and brain. Still, I needed to know the gist for legal and perhaps literary reasons (I was naturally contemplating a book), so I commissioned a sweet-natured pal, William—who'd worked as an editor for a New York newspaper and was adept at circumspect summary—to break down each major article in terms of (1) cooperating sources, (2) notable quotes, and (3) "salient bits" (often paraphrased).

"Mr. Bailey's Class"—the *Slate* piece that appeared April 29, 2021, about my years teaching at Lusher magnet school in New Orleans—would seem the best source for the grooming narrative, insofar as it allows for the faint possibility that I might be an actual human being with complicated motives. "Nearly everyone we spoke to said Mr. Bailey was one of the best teachers they'd ever had," *Slate* reported. I was glad to know that my old students, now in their thirties and forties, still remember me as "funny, charismatic, and academically demanding," that I expected them "to read challenging books, and to think independently," even while I "cursed in front of them, told off-color jokes, and acknowledged the existence of sex":

> . . . His love of literature, his delight at the power of words, his interest in his middle schoolers' growth— all of that was obvious to everyone at Lusher, kids and adults. Steve Burt, a now-retired Lusher English teacher, saw Mr. Bailey's work ethic and charisma up close. "A lot of his students would gather around him like a little flock on field trips, and he'd entertain them with witty banter," Burt says. "It wasn't unwholesome. It was kind of nice to see."

Steve was a nice guy with a fun, full life outside of teaching (which I couldn't quite say for myself at the time), so he kept an amiable distance from most of his colleagues, including me. In short, he and I weren't close; maybe that's why he could afford to be generous later. Quoting Kinbote in *Pale Fire* (*not* the Nabokov novel I'm most associated with), I say this about Steve Burt: "Let there appear for a moment his hand and mine firmly clasping each other across the water over the golden wake of an emblematic sun."

The nicer parts of the *Slate* piece reminded me of why I used to love being a teacher—particularly those seven years at Lusher, when I taught so many smart kids on the touching cusp of adulthood, so eager to learn about "morality and death and love," as *Slate* notes. Good old Jackie D.—who once got an ungovernable fit of the giggles during a test-prep class I taught after school for extra money, until she poured onto the floor and I had to drag her slowly out of the room by her enormous book bag (still attached to her shoulders)—told *Slate* that I "just landed deus ex machina" (a term we'd discussed) "in our class to teach us what it means to be intellectual." It also pleases me to know, thanks to *Slate*, that my student Katie F. thinks I'm part of the reason she got two English degrees and went on to be a writer and teacher herself. Also noted by *Slate*—as an instance of how devoted and vaguely sinister (both) I was—were my students' dialogue journals, which I studied "with the same ardor [I'd] later apply to the personal papers of Richard Yates, John Cheever, and Philip Roth." Sure, why not? And yes, I'd doodle in the margins with my red pens, and sometimes encourage them to be more confiding than what was strictly appropriate. But they delighted me, and truth be known I was lonely then—still a writer manqué, a lonely business at any time, and just lonely period: I wouldn't marry until the summer after my last year at Lusher (2000), and meanwhile I had my bachelor thirties to slog through.

"Nobody cared as much as Mr. Bailey did," said *Slate*,

though I'm sure the dark side of that formulation was given equal time and more—namely, as my first rape accuser (of two), Eve P., put it: I only *really* "cared about what [I] could get from" my students once they were no longer minors. But more about Eve in a bit.

Meanwhile I hope the reader will accept that I wasn't sexually attracted to Sam B., whom I loved and who loved me. Sam was my brightest male pupil, popular with girls and boys alike, who were all aware that Sam's older brother had killed himself the year before (just as Eve P.'s had killed himself; just as mine killed himself a decade later), and needed and deserved a lot of kindness. One day I read aloud Raymond Carver's "A Small, Good Thing" about the death of a little boy and his parents' efforts to cope with it; when I came to the part where Howard, the father, embraces his dead son's bicycle, Sam put a hand over his face, very discreetly, but otherwise controlled himself. As *Slate* acknowledges, Sam was one of my "most eager correspondents" via his journal:

> He hungered for his teacher's intellectual and social guidance, at times using his journal to pose questions to Mr. Bailey directly. There could be a tenderness to the teacher's responses. Mr. Bailey urged Sam to be less spiteful and a better friend to a classmate who was struggling. He told his student to visit Europe after high school graduation and to read Salinger's *Franny and Zooey* "all the way through" [since, after all, it's about two siblings trying to process a beloved older brother's suicide]. And he quoted the Max Ehrmann

poem "Desiderata": "With all its sham, drudgery, and broken dreams, it is still a beautiful world."

I didn't know "Desiderata" was the work of one Max Ehrmann, but I always believed in those last lines (still do, more or less). *Slate* characterizes me, qua teacher, as a "wise" (if wily) "older brother," and I won't deny I tried to fill such a role for Sam and certain others who seemed to welcome it. For most of his eighth-grade year, Sam was sick with love for a fellow student who didn't quite reciprocate, and *Slate* reminds me that I wrote a full-page red-ink response in Sam's journal about how I myself had been "'liberated' from years of infatuation with one young woman . . . after a single kiss around Christmas time." (I don't remember writing as much to Sam, but I certainly remember that Christmas kiss.) *Slate*: "'This would have been a huge day for me when he wrote this,' Sam says now, looking back over his journal. A sprawling comment from Mr. Bailey gave Sam the 'feeling of being heard.'" I last saw Sam in 2014, when I was fifty and he was thirty-four; I was in town for the Tennessee Williams Literary Festival, and we lunched with another of my students from Sam's year, Kevin M. That year's festival was also the occasion for a last, friendly, in-person chat with Eve P.—over a single drink at the Monteleone bar—eleven years after the episode she'd later characterize as rape.

With very little exception that I can recall, it was up to my former students to stay in touch with me while they were minors. Arguably the Lusher student I was closest to—certainly the one I saw and heard from most over the years—was Martha*: the only one of my students who ever had the audacity to phone me at home, at whatever hour, just to chat; while she was my student I let the machine pick up, though later, when she was in high school and beyond, we'd often have long, idle chats about everything and nothing. I was friends with her mother, a divorced woman somewhat older than myself, who encouraged me to visit Martha in her room and listen to her music and/or talk her out of her funks. I'm pretty sure I never set foot in the bedrooms of my other students or ex-students—or anyway hung out there, as I did with Martha—whether or not I was friends with their parents. Martha and I made mix tapes for each other (she was pointedly unimpressed with mine), chatted about our various family woes, and yes, talked a little about sex— or rather Martha would occasionally confide, morosely, about some boy she'd been with, though I can't recall ever reciprocating with a tale from my own life, maybe because Martha was mostly interested in herself. And that was fine.

Martha was pretty in a freckle-faced, bleary-eyed way, her chopped-up hair sometimes sprayed purple or green in places, banded in random rattails or just quietly allowed to sprawl. She was deeply lovable, and when she was away, visiting her dad in the DC area, I missed her. But as she'll tell you, I never made the vaguest hint of a play for her, and we continued to meet now and then until she was in her late-twenties. (During our last in-person chat, she turned around and carefully, non-provocatively peeled the back of

* Not her real name. I permit myself to use the first names of former students/ accusers only when they themselves have publicly seen fit to do so. Otherwise I use pseudonyms.

her shirt up to show me the lurid tattoos covering every square inch of her skin.) Whatever was in the air between us, it wasn't that; quite simply I had nobody else in my life like her and didn't want to jeopardize our oddball bond. If only I'd behaved with the same consideration toward certain other, also-quite-lovable (each in her own way) ex-students, but too late. When the shit hit the fan in 2021, Martha left a message on my phone (wondering whether I wanted to talk), I left one on hers (not just at the moment, thanks, but maybe later), and we left it at that.

Chapter Seven

OUR FUCKED-UP FAMILY

When I think of my father's eminence as a lawyer, I'm reminded of that line from *My Dinner with Andre* (misattributed, if one goes by the Criterion Collection subtitles, to Bergman's *Autumn Sonata*): "I could always live in my art, but never in my life." Burck's life was far from a botch, but outside of his profession/art he rarely seemed (to me) quite comfortable in his own chameleonic skin, and he was certainly bewildered by his bad luck in the domestic sphere. "When I think of my family over the years," he noted in 2011, "I think it is my biggest failure, but I don't know what I would have done differently—that's probably an indictment of me."

In 1987, while staying with his second wife at a monastery in New Mexico, Burck wrote a long, soul-searching

letter to my twenty-six-year-old brother, Scott, whose life
had been one goddamn thing after another—drinking,
drugs, car wrecks, rehab, jail, etc.—for at least a decade by
then. Burck noted that his bad marriage had had something
to do with his failures as a young parent, plus of course he'd
always been too caught up in his work.

> But nothing accounts for the sorry job of fathering
> that I did through your early years. (I think I improved
> somewhat in later years and I'll write about that in due
> course.) I think you will be inclined to disagree with
> my dark assessment of my performance as a father.
> There is something in nature that makes the offspring
> too forgiving and too bonded to the idea of superior-
> ity in their parents. But I know, on this point if on no
> other, that my assessment is at least close to the truth.
> It is the single most bitter truth that I have to confront
> about myself. . . . So, for my sins of commission and
> omission, I ask forgiveness.

I can assure Burck, from this side of the grave, that my
late brother certainly did *not* disagree with Burck's "dark
assessment of [his] performance as a father," though Scott's
love for Burck would always be vast if tortured. In fact, he
sent me a copy of Burck's 1987 apologia (Burck would also
send me a copy many years later) with some such gloss
as *About time he admitted what a shitty father he was*. But
of course Scott was always casting about for any extenua-
tion of his own colossal fuckups—which, by the way, Burck
went on to tabulate exhaustively in that *mea*-not-so-*culpa*

from the monastery. He could never resist indulging in a strong degree of advocacy on his own behalf and/or that of his clients.

But maybe Scott was reading Burck's letter in the right spirit after all: rereading it now, after many years, I notice that Burck is, in fact, rather careful to blame himself ("perhaps the injury was done so early that I didn't know it") while ticking off that laundry list of disasters in my brother's life. "My behavior in letting things unravel like they did is inexplicable to me now," Burck wrote.

> . . . It is now nine years ago that you graduated from high school. Nine years of mostly darkness and trauma for you. I see you on the night of your graduation—long hair and that unpleasant expression that instantly antagonizes virtually everyone who meets or sees you—the only person in the procession who doesn't wear the mortarboard but carries it swinging along instead. I can still feel the rush of blood to my face as I blush.

How distinctly I picture "that unpleasant expression" my father means, Scott's default face whenever he felt angry or threatened or airily amused or something of all three, usually while stoned and of course he was stoned most of the time, and my God *yes*, the mortification of being recognized in public as this abysmal creep's father or brother. I knew it only too well.

In *Splendid* I recount an episode from that last nightmare summer before Scott left for college at NYU—when our father brought him home from jail in the middle of the night, stoned out of his gourd, whereupon Scott stood in my doorway taunting me ("You're gonna be just like me . . .") rather than go contritely to bed, until my mortally exhausted father had to throw him out of the house. I often reflect on that low point (among many) of my early ado-lescence, but reading about it from Burck's point of view, in his letter, I realize to what extent I'd been spared the worst. Scott had been arrested that night while racing his motorcycle along the wrong side of May Avenue, one of the busiest thoroughfares in Oklahoma City. "The police called me at midnight and I hurried over," Burck wrote. "You were out of your mind, as I had so often seen, on PCP or some such poison. I have heard the cursing and dirty talk of low and vulgar people many times in my life, but I have never, before or since, heard anyone speak the filth that came from your mouth that night. I thought if I wasn't there, the police officer would kill Scott and make it look like an accident."

He also wrote about Scott dropping out of NYU, a month or so later, when I saw Burck cry for the first time (of two) in our lives. Again I'm struck, rereading it now, by how much Burck stressed his own culpability:

> . . . you went off to NYU. I remember with remorse how relieved I was to have you far away. Hope is truly perennial as the grass, and I have indulged in repeated and almost boundless hope where you are concerned. When you left for New York, I hoped that the excitement and adventure [such as Burck himself

had felt circa 1958] would press you upward and out of the terrible abyss of your suffering. But all too soon I got your call—you were dropping out of college. I wept like a baby . . . I am ashamed of myself for shipping you off to college like you were some package to be casually dropped at the post office. In retrospect I can't imagine me doing that—it further evidences the difficulties and distance between us. . . . I corresponded with the psychologist at NYU who had seen you while you were there—neither that professional nor any other was ever able to tell me anything that made sense to me.

Amen. A number of people remarked, deploringly or not, that my memoir failed to posit any definite explanation for my brother's wayward behavior. I wasn't silent on the point out of some modernist impulse of ambiguity; I simply don't know. My wife, a superb psychologist, didn't know either; she agreed he didn't really fit into any DSM pigeonhole and wasn't a paranoid schizophrenic (as one of his psychiatrists opined) given that he suffered, at least in sober moments, only the everyday self-deception of addicts and failures everywhere, versus, say, lurid delusions about transistors in his brain or whatever.

Also in my memoir I mention Burck's attempt to bring Scott home from New York before the drugs and whatever else killed him, and now I see that Burck had made at least *three* such attempts. (Scott eventually came home, alone, via a bus for which Burck had bought the ticket.) But then, Burck's way of talking about Scott over the years—especially after Scott died—was so sporadic and elliptical that I might be excused for conflating bits and pieces of the whole repetitive nightmare. "When, after a long time, I went to New York to see you," Burck wrote in his letter, "I was aghast at the sight of this stranger—glazed eyes, unkempt and unclean. Your talk was irrational and deluded." I wonder whether that was the time Scott talked about founding a Utopian society on the bottom of the sea (as I wrote in my book), or the time he insisted, stoned, on bringing a stray cat aboard the plane back to Oklahoma—an episode Burck only mentioned once, in his cups, after my memoir had been published. That latter episode (cat) must have constituted his *third* failed attempt to bring Scott home, since, according to his 1987 monastery letter, he'd also left empty-handed after his second attempt:

> When I next came to New York to see you, it was worse—you had deteriorated mentally and physically and I despaired of you ever getting well. You were friendless, as usual—but worse yet, you weren't even on decent terms with another human being. I came to that depressing room where you "lived" one afternoon and you were incomprehensibly muttering on the bed. I couldn't get you to come to. On the floor were some small pages of paper where you had written of your anguish and contemplation of suicide. There were also love poems and they were very tender and sweet and, I thought, better than most of what I see published. I picked up the notes and took them, as being all of you there was left. Later, upon re-reading

them for the 20th time, they became too painful and I destroyed them.

BURCK'S REMORSE OVER Scott, at least in retrospect, was surely mixed up with his not-very-wholesome marriage to my mother. I must have been ten or eleven when my parents and I were watching a TV show that touched on some act of adultery, and I remember asking them what I thought was a rhetorical question:

"You guys would never kiss other people like that, would you?"

When they stopped laughing, I think it was Burck who gently explained that even in the best marriages these days it was hardly expected for either partner to be confined by such antiquated notions of . . . blah blah, whatever. I can't remember what he said, only my surprise and faint dismay over the dimly understood implications.

An open marriage in the seventies was not that big a deal, of course, though I daresay it was an anomaly in most pockets of middle-class Oklahoma. Eventually I think Marlies would have insisted on a degree of sexual latitude whatever the zeitgeist, and my father would have gone along because, well, that's what he wanted, too—indeed it went to the heart of whatever bond he had with my mother, whom he'd married, in part, to distance himself from his boring provincial origins. Not long ago I was going through my mother's personal things—I'd just moved her into an assisted-living facility—and found a cache of nude photos she and Burck had taken of each other on our back porch when, presumably,

Scott and I were elsewhere. (Not that our presence would have been all that inhibiting. Once, when I was a kid, Burck blithely doffed Marlies's bikini top and took her boob into his mouth while I stood in the pool watching. I think she laughed and pushed him away after a moment or two.) Looking at the photos, I was struck by (1) how much they seem to be enjoying themselves, and (2) what good bodies they still had in their forties.

Around that time they took a "movie cruise" in the Caribbean—the actor Glenn Ford and various other lesser lights were aboard—and the photos again suggest they had a great time. A redheaded gamine named Marcie appears in a lot of these photos, and her Hollywood headshot was framed on my parents' bedroom wall for a while afterward. She was a starlet who appeared in the odd pilot episode I watched with my parents, though her career never really took off as far as I can tell. Anyway my mother likes to reminisce about the time Marcie confided an attraction to Marlies's dashing, prosperous husband, and the two women conspired to bring things to fruition . . . not that Burck needed much persuading. Marlies was sunning herself on the deck while Marcie and my father were taking advantage of their empty cabin; when Marcie reappeared, alone, my mother gave her an inquiring look, and Marcie laughed and went elaborately bowlegged to indicate how vigorously she'd just been shagged.

GIVEN HOW THINGS soured between us after his second marriage, it's easy to forget just how companionable Burck

and I were in those early years, how quick he was to praise
and protect me. Even his incidental censure was leavened
with humor. He kept a portable tape recorder on his person
or in his glove compartment at all times—mostly for stray
thoughts relating to his work—and when I remarked that
I planned to groom my long dirty hair a bit more scrupu-
lously once I was older, my father benignly inquired how
much older. "When I'm fifteen?" I ventured—whereupon he
reached into his glove compartment and pressed Record:
"Remind Blake, on his fifteenth birthday, to get a haircut."
Another time, a few years later, I sheepishly admitted that
I had a rather nasty pustule on the underside of my penis
and good reason to worry about its provenance. In a sober
voice, without pause, Burck suggested amputation, which in
retrospect doesn't seem a bad idea.

We played a lot of chess, beginning when I was eight or
so, and maybe a year passed before I managed to win a game.
My father would always murmur "checkmate" with marked
sorrow before carefully explaining what I might have done
differently. God knows I needed mollification, since I was
(am) a grotesque loser. I sometimes cried and threw tan-
trums, only the worst of which Burck would rebuke—bearing in mind, perhaps, that I came by my D-minus temperament honestly: the progeny of Burck *and* Marlies, after all.
Witness that first chess victory of mine, while we were in
Germany visiting my grandparents: Burck had made a bad
move and taken his hand off the piece for less than a second, but I wouldn't let him take it back (as bad a winner as
a loser), and when I flung up my arms in victory, he dashed
the pieces off the board and stormed away . . . only to

return a minute later and beg forgiveness from his shocked and sobbing nine-year-old son. He was always abject after his blowups.

I'm sure he was under a terrible strain in those days, for all sorts of reasons, and even at the best of times I think the lava was churning away beneath the surface. For all my own volatility, I rarely lapsed into the kind of weird everyday peevishness that Burck allowed himself when nobody was looking, so to speak. Just off the top of my head: Once, he thrust an arm between elevator doors to keep them from closing so that a rushing woman could breathlessly enter; when she stared at the floor and declined to thank him, Burck bent his face toward hers and gave her a hard, menacing stare for the duration of the ride. Thus (you may say) a lesson in common courtesy for a rude stranger, but my main impression was of his morbid *amour-propre*. And I think this also relates to his out-of-the-blue meannesses toward me when I was older—about my Yates book, say— at a time, that is, when he could no longer manhandle his grownup son but had to blow off steam one way or the other.

And still one returns, as one must, to his essential sweetness. When Scott began to go off the rails, Burck worked harder at their relationship without, however, tolerating his older son's tendency to take out his frustrations on me via vicious mockery and/or outright violence. One day Burck sat me down and sweetly explained that he was going to Grand Lake for his twenty-fifth high school reunion, for which he could only take one of his kids and had decided to take Scott because of his seniority or whatever. Of course

I began to cry: he was *always* doing things with Scott, I complained—taking him along when he went to his office on Saturdays, throwing the football with him, etc. Burck was listening gravely to this *cri de coeur* when Scott walked in on us and promptly mocked me as a crybaby—"*Aye-lie-lie!*"—whereupon Burck bolted to his feet and commanded Scott to unpack his own bag because he was staying home. "*Now* look who's crying!" I wanted to say but didn't, lest Burck change his mind again.

As it happened I was probably a better choice as traveling companion, given Burck's main *raison* for this anomalous sentimental journey: namely, to get his ashes hauled with a former Vinita High sweetheart, now the boozy single mom of a *very* goofy son for whom I was expected to serve as playmate. We were both thirteen, the son and I, and mostly I remember whiling away the weekend in a pool, bemused, as the kid regaled me about certain esoteric aspects of old *Star Trek* episodes and the like. (Later he joined a cult and disappeared from his mother's life, at least for a while and perhaps forever.) Suffice it to say the erotic side of Burck's trip would have been badly compromised if I hadn't come along to distract the goofy son, whom my older brother would have bullied or shunned or both. In later years, I'd occasionally remind Burck of this strange caper, and he always seemed surprised that I'd figured out his raffish intentions toward the old girlfriend; then I'd remind him of the goofy son and my wingman role in keeping the latter occupied. "Oh yeah," Burck would say, with a low whistle, recalling the son's later cult membership and perhaps sparing a thought for the boozy mom too.

Chapter Eight

ALL ABOUT EVE

In the course of my final email exchange with Eve P. in the summer of 2020—seventeen years after the episode she'd later characterize as rape—she deviated a little from her usual conviviality to mention that her older daughter was about to enter eighth-grade at Lusher, where the daughter, like her mother twenty-seven years before, would have a male English teacher: "I care about you and enjoy corresponding with you (I always have and likely always will)," Eve wrote, "and you were a tremendous influence in my life . . . but not all of my memories of you are necessarily good ones. So. That's been weird." I replied that the memory to which she was mainly alluding (albeit not yet as an act of rape) had occurred in 2003, when she was in her twenties and I in my thirties, almost a full decade after her eighth-grade year. "[Bailey's] email"—i.e., the one

I just paraphrased—"also claimed he was suffering from an unspecified mental illness at the time of the [2003] encounter," the *Times-Picayune* reported on April 20, 2021.

I stand by that diagnosis. The episode in question—a very strange caper indeed—occurred in mid-June 2003, a couple of weeks before my Yates biography was published. Scott had killed himself two months before, news of which I received the same Easter weekend I was informed that my third book proposal in a row had been declined by my publisher, Picador. That meant I would have to get another teaching job, and quickly, or else we'd have to subsist on my wife's grad-school stipend, and we couldn't subsist on that. As for my Yates biography: I'd been very pleased with the two hundred thousand-word book I'd managed to produce in the fourteen months Picador had stipulated, and my editor had professed to like it, but given their brisk dismissal of my subsequent proposals, not to mention my once-promising brother's suicide, I was feeling pretty depressed and bewildered about things. Again, I'd been faithful to my wife during the first three years of our marriage preceding the incident with Eve, and for what it's worth I claim my behavior that night was less a carnal impulse than a dotty and *very* improper attempt to console myself with a kindred spirit: Eve, too, after all, had lost an older brother to suicide; what's more, her brother was also named Scott.

Along with "Mr. Bailey's Class" on April 29, 2021, *Slate* published Eve's separate account of our relationship and the episode in 2003. "I simply don't know what possesses me sometimes," I emailed Eve (so quoted in *Slate*). "Nothing to say, really, except 'sorry' over and over." What I was

apologizing for was an unseemly pass at a former student—
my first-ever as a married man, and bewildering for both
Eve and me, all the more because of the almost total lack
of context, chemistry, rhyme/reason, what you will. "When
[Mr. Bailey] asked me to go back with him to the place
where he was staying, I really didn't expect anything would
happen," Eve wrote in *Slate*. "In fact, when he kissed me,
my first reaction was to laugh because it was so bizarre
to me that *Mr. Bailey* had just kissed me. I think I was in
complete shock as the rest of it unfolded." That makes two
of us. We'd been having a drink at a dingy Uptown New
Orleans bar, and I remember splitting into two, so to speak,
as we got up to go: (1) the stunned, deploring observer,
wondering what the hell his (2) corporeal counterpart was
doing kissing *Eve* of all people, who was about to marry her
first husband. "Do you want to go home, or do you want
to go to my place?" I asked her, per Antioch Rules, and it
proceeded like that: "Do you want to stay here" (the front
room of my friend's pied-à-terre), "or do you want to go to the
bedroom?" We were out of our clothes and recumbent—but
not having sex—when Eve said in a woebegone way, "This
is wrong on so many levels." Whereupon my Observing Self
gained, belatedly, but not too belatedly, the upper hand; I
remember the tremendous relief I felt when I realized I was
not, after all, going to engage in a stupid, gratuitous act of
adultery with a soon-to-be-married woman who moreover
was a former student.

When my lawyer—a smart, worldly, good-natured graduate of UVA Law—responded to allegations in the two *Slate*
articles of April 29, 2021, he was mostly thinking of Eve

when he observed, "These complainants kept up longstanding, friendly relationships with Mr. Bailey for many years. These relationships—between highly educated, intelligent adults—occurred long after the supposed assaults occurred, and they are not the type of friendships that anyone would have with someone who raped or abused them." By then I'd provided him with a highly selective winnowing (four or five single-spaced pages) from Eve's many emails to me during the years *after* the episode in 2003, often signed with "Love" or "xo" and including photos of her children.

Toward the end of her *Slate* piece, Eve referred to our final email exchange in the summer of 2020, when she'd mentioned how she felt "weird" about her daughter's eighth-grade teacher being a man—like me—whereupon I replied that such reminders of my long-ago bad behavior were unnerving, to put it mildly. Eve quoted her response in *Slate*: "'You're not a monster; I wouldn't stay in touch if I believed that,' I wrote, trying to console him. 'And I know you were not yourself, and I know you've apologized. . . . But it definitely fucked me up for a long time and certainly shatters my well-being when I recall it, as well.'" My editor-friend William transcribed the passage thus, and I asked him whether that ellipsis after "apologized" was Eve's/*Slate*'s or his. It was Eve's; in her original email of July 28, 2020, there's a comma after "apologized," and what follows (elided in *Slate*) is this: ". . . and I hope you know I've forgiven you and accepted my own share of blame in the whole mess." Then, after the sentence that follows the ellipsis in *Slate* ("But it definitely fucked me up," etc.), she wrote this in her original email (also elided in *Slate*): "I think it's fair to categorize our relationship as 'it's complicated,' as Facebook would have it. Also believe me, <u>it wasn't just you</u>. You were just the one I cared about most."

The underlined phrase was hyperlinked to a blog post she'd written "at the height of #MeToo"—a few lightly fictionalized vignettes about various mentors who'd proved to be "interested in [her] body only": none of these vignettes involves sex (much less rape) or anything worse than creepy flirtation; my own cameo is based on my exchange with Eve after she'd received a high school writing award in 1997, and conflates my actual flattery ("Great genius is always going to be lonely") with what I'd allegedly said, in 2003, about wanting her "since the day we met." Two other vignettes feature a French teacher who gives the twelve-year-old Eve a piece of chocolate and rubs her shoulders "in a way that isn't entirely inappropriate but definitely leaves you feeling extraordinarily confused and weirded out," as well as a high school PE teacher who claims she has promise as a runner, only to remark "Man, I love watching you jiggle" while she obligingly circles the track. "These situations leave you wondering: *Am* I any good at French? *Am* I a gifted writer? *Do* I actually have decent form as a runner? . . . It all gets tangled up with how much you *want* to believe these things about yourself."

I don't think Eve cared all that much about her French or running prowess, but she most definitely cared about whether or not she was a gifted writer, as I'd repeatedly led her to believe. "Mr. V—— definitely was a perv," she wrote me on July 28, 2020, re the real-life model for her shoulder-rubbing French teacher—in other words, he was even worse than her eighth-grade English teacher ("I'm not calling you a perv or anything like that"), whom she would accuse of rape less than a year later.

Chapter Nine

RETURN TO VINITA VALUES

When my Aunt Kay told me about Burck's youthful predilection for redheads, then casually observed that his second wife, Sandra, resembled nobody so much as the woman he'd thrown over for Marlies, the red-headed Lydia, I muttered a little epiphanic "Huh!" I thought of Gatsby ("Can't repeat the past? Why of course you can!"); I thought of Jimmy Stewart gazing at the reincarnated Kim Novak in *Vertigo*. Of course it's possible the physical resemblance was just a coincidence, but I haven't the least doubt that Burck—by marrying Sandra Barnett of Garden City, Kansas—was roundly disavowing his blunder of twenty years before.

"The biggest change in my life came when I met and married Sandra," Burck wrote in 2011 (among the same notes wherein he reflects that family was "the biggest failure" in his life). "She taught me how to have fun, how to enjoy life, how to act silly, how to be more outgoing."

Speaking only for myself, I found the Burck of my childhood a lot more fun (if problematic in other ways) than the man he became after marrying Sandra. Consider Sandra's immediate predecessor, the young woman I call Mandy in my previous memoir: she was a law student clerking for Burck's firm—exactly half his age: twenty-three to his forty-six; as Burck would fondly recall in later years, she liked to wear light summer dresses loosely fastened with a sash, the better to flash her full-frontal nudity at my father as they passed in the hall, a cue for him to go wait in his office, where she'd shortly appear, lock the door, and blow him under his desk. Now, I call that fun.

I was seventeen, and the first time I met Mandy was when I spotted her with my father (still technically married to my mother) on a downtown sidewalk. I knew immediately, ding dong, that they were shagging each other. Burck all but winked at me when he introduced the dimpled Mandy, who seemed delighted to meet any son of this marvelous man, then off they went tittering like a couple of school kids. Our subsequent meeting, when Burck brought her home that first time (Marlies was mostly living in Norman by then, taking college classes and shagging a nice grad student named Bob), was even happier: they caught me in a rare mood of virtue, doing the dishes *and* listening to classical music. Mandy seemed impressed, and we became pals for the duration of her attachment to my father—this despite my having to take long walks, visit friends, and so on, whenever she was around, i.e., having noisy sex with Burck.

My first meeting with Sandra was also a proper augury for the relationship that followed. I was watching dumb TV in my boxers when Burck, without warning, blew in with his new lady friend. His pained look on introducing us— thin lips, furrowed brow—seemed out of proportion to my TV-boxers combo, whereas Sandra's smile looked like a wire about to snap. I tried to make things go with a bit of chitchat, but they quickly made an excuse to leave. Alone again, I went to the bathroom and the mirror reminded me that I'd applied a few garish white globs of pimple cream to the minefield on my forehead. I couldn't help reflecting that my face had been relatively clear when Mandy had visited that first time; on the other hand, if Sandra had encountered that zit-less, dishwashing, Ravel-listening paragon (so I observe, sadder but wiser, forty-plus years down the road), she might have been even *more* disposed to loathe me, especially once she learned that the dishwashing part was deceptive to say the least.

For a while, though, we both tried hard, and nowadays I'm inclined to give Sandra more credit and myself less. And I was far from the only vexing aspect of her life with my father. There was Scott, of course, who deserves a separate book (and got it), but what about Burck's former wife, who had every intention of staying friends with Burck (whom she still called *Bäbsch*, a mashup of Burck, Papa, and Schätzchen) and assumed that his later wives and/or lovers would be nothing but delighted to make friends with her. "There was an enthusiastic knock on my door the other day," she wrote Burck from Norman, two years after his marriage to Sandra, "and in bounces ole [Mandy], freshly graduated from OU law school. . . . we thought we'd have a picture made for you anyway—in fond remembrance of times past." The enclosed photo showed the two women embracing on an unmade bed and coquettishly toasting the camera with flutes of Champagne.

But Mandy was no Sandra, who once found a little note Marlies had secreted in Burck's medicine cabinet during one of her furtive visits: "What's this? *Suppositories?* Since when have *you* needed suppositories . . . ?" How best to explain Sandra's enduring outrage? Her thoughts went something like this: Where did this woman—this *ex-wife*—get off letting herself into a house that was no longer hers and leaving kittenish notes for a man no longer her husband, notes adverting to a bodily function, moreover, that is noisome and *private*? Burck himself, when trying to explain a key difference in his relations with Sandra versus Marlies, liked to point out that Sandra would (at most) diffidently tap on a closed bathroom door and say her little piece ("Burck, dinner's ready"), whereas Marlies would barge right in, make some cackling remark about the stench (poor Burck's chronic diarrhea), then proceed to brush her teeth or whatever else while he sheepishly finished his business.

I know Sandra took a dim view of that little note about suppositories because she told me so—this during an exhaustive harangue about Marlies's *many* lapses, imparted at a time, early in our relationship, when Sandra and I still hoped we'd be great chums. I don't think I took any particular offense, but rather conceded to Sandra that my mother *was* a handful, if a basically well-meaning handful (my opinion unto the present day). I think I understood that Sandra needed a confidant for such sorrows, and who better than the young man who'd endured eighteen years of Marlies's dubious parenting? Thus I listened patiently to the whole spiel, at pains not to betray a filial loyalty I scarcely felt. Sandra, however, on reflection, decided it was in poor taste to blackguard a young man's mother to his face and wrote me a very apologetic *what-was-I-thinking?* note and left it in my sock drawer.

Would that I had shown the same sensitivity toward Sandra when, say, her decrepit little poodle went missing a week or so after she and her kids had moved in with Burck and me. The poodle had clearly been on her last pegs, pissing all over the rugs and looking generally peaked.

"I couldn't find her," sighed Sandra on returning.

"Did you look?" said I.

"Yes, Blake, I did."

And she slammed a door between us. Rightly so.

Let's jump ahead eighteen years—to early 2000, the better to elide the long deterioration of my relations with Sandra, not to say the dull grind of my apprenticeship as a writer. My last-ever completed novel had been good enough to interest a literary agent but not good enough to sell, so the agent advised me to write a book proposal (nonfiction) about whatever interested me at the moment. Though I'd never remotely pictured myself as a biographer, I was intensely curious about Richard Yates, who'd written two of the best postwar American novels, *Revolutionary Road* and *The Easter Parade*, and two great story collections, *Eleven Kinds of Loneliness* and *Liars in Love*—and yet his books were completely out of print and he himself was dead and mostly forgotten. Long story short: I got in touch with his middle daughter, Monica, who told me (among other things) that her late father had been (1) bipolar and a pioneering consumer of psychotropic drugs, (2) RFK's sole speechwriter at the height of the Civil Rights Movement, and (3) the model for Elaine Benes's surly novelist father in a 1990 *Seinfeld* episode, "The Jacket," based on a meeting in the mid-eighties between Yates and the show's co-creator, Larry David, who was dating Monica at the time.

My agent liked the Yates proposal and considered it salable—it helped that a new Vintage paperback of *Revolutionary Road* was about to be published that spring, with an introduction by Richard Ford that also appeared in the *New York Times Book Review*—which was one of the reasons I quit teaching while waiting to get married that summer. When my proposal finally sold, in January 2001, my wife and I had almost run through my $11,000 pension money from the Orleans Parish school system and were due to subsist on my wife's grad-student stipend of $700 a month plus the dregs of a four-figure advance (minus agent commission) I'd received on signing my contract with Picador. I tried to make the most of my remaining time and money. While visiting Boston to pore over Yates's papers, I stayed at a hostel that put me in mind of a pirate ship: in the bunks on either side of me were a big snoring Asian guy and a Swede in bikini briefs; our other roommates were harder to descry in the murky darkness, though I'm pretty sure one of them was masturbating. Meanwhile I was working twelve-hour days and only pausing to eat, sleep, and defecate. With the best will in the world, though, I'd almost run out of money—my pension *and* royalty advance—by November 2001, or roughly four months before I was expected to deliver my finished book to Picador.

Naturally I turned to my father—but "squeamishly," don't you know: "You had no reason to expect, thirty-eight years ago," I wrote him, "that your son would still have times of financial dependence . . ." Given my lamentable history of sponging, I can almost hear Burck's heavy sigh while mulling my latest ingenious proposal for paying him back: If he would take out a loan of about, oh, $10,000, in his name, my wife and I would make payments on it once I'd received the balance of my royalty advance and also (my agent assured me) the proceeds of a magazine sale ("a definite person at the *New Yorker* is interested"), and so on. "After that, Picador has optioned my next book, which they will buy in proposal form unless they don't, in which case I'll get a teaching job in the fall."

"I was overwhelmed by your generous offer to help Blake and me financially," my wife wrote Burck, after he'd given us the money and ruled out repayment. "We are both working hard, as usual. Blake never takes a day off—even got up before dawn Thanksgiving morning to write." Which was only the truth.

BY THE SPRING of 2003 it appeared that my virtuous work ethic would have to be its own reward. My Yates book was due to be published that summer, but meanwhile Picador had rejected two of my subsequent proposals and would reject the third (six months of work) on Good Friday— the same day, it so happened, that my brother was found unresponsive in his cell at the Oklahoma County Jail. His bedsheet was knotted around his neck, and his death was ruled a suicide, though it's possible he'd been murdered by a guard or fellow inmate, since he was hardly one to sow goodwill in such places. As Marlies had written about one of her prison visits with Scott, "He looks like Rasputin, long hair, spindly beard, and emaciated to a stick. I am very worried about him. Someone punched him in the mouth, and his lip was cut and his nose swollen. He thinks he's in danger, and kept telling me to investigate his death, if anything should happen to him."

Though I wept and still occasionally weep for Scott, my quiet opinion was that he—or whoever his murderer was—did himself and his loved ones a favor. Now we could focus on remembering him as the often delightful, precocious youngster he'd been, and let his evil be interred with his bones. Making peace with our tortured memories of Scott was the main point of a little memorial service Marlies had planned at her pet cemetery in the country, though Burck bristled when I urged him (during one of our morning car-phone chats) to attend.

"Well," he said gruffly, "I may or may not, son."

I didn't have the moral authority to wrestle with him much, on this or any other subject, but I tried to convey in so many words that it would be better for Burck's own peace of mind, going forward, to take part in the obsequies, whereas Burck wanted me to know (also in so many words) that he'd abundantly paid his dues where Scott was concerned, and *nobody* (least of all me) would tell him how to mourn that changeling pain in the ass. Such cussedness, I reflected, was more intrinsic to Burck than perhaps any other aspect of his character: it lurked in the long impervious silences of our perennial estrangements, and (casting ahead) in his refusal to let me visit or help until the very last days of his dying. He alone was Captain of his Soul, and that was fucking *that*.

In the end he showed up at Scott's little funeral, kept a vague stoical smile afloat, then slipped away for a long solitary walk afterward.

A SOMBER MOOD still prevailed when I visited him at Breeze Hill (his opulent 325-acre ranch near Chandler, OK) a couple weeks later. That was the time I handed him a freshly minted copy of my Yates biography, which he handled like a cumbersome turd, then made that crack about my "two and a half inches of posterity." I responded with a sort of sickly giggle, but Burck gave me a look to let me know he wasn't kidding. I was a little dizzy with swallowed rage, and sometimes I wonder how it might have affected my future—for better and for worse—if I'd allowed myself the catharsis of telling him to go fuck himself. But I just giggled and let it go.

Burck was drinking more in his old age, and that's the first time I can remember ever getting drunk with him. (Sandra was elsewhere—at a periodic gathering of her old high school clique, the Holy Eight, so known because of their staunch virginity and exalted popularity. I was told there'd also been an Unholy Nine at Garden City High, and I wished them well.) At some point we broached the subject of adultery, a sin whereof I'd yet to be guilty after three years of marriage. Maybe I was only being kittenish when I asked Burck whether *he'd* strayed during his twenty-plus years with Sandra, but he somberly fanned a hand between us.

"Never. Never. You *have* to be faithful. It's the only way."

"Not even an occasional . . . ?"

More hand-fanning and head-shaking. I gave him a little smile meant to remind him of his first marriage—the context of my childhood—but his hand seemed to wield an eraser to those years.

"Only when a marriage has become a joke—a *joke*—unworthy of the name," he said, reading my smile correctly. "You *have* to be faithful."

Thus the model husband and pillar of the community counseled me. And of course I would have done well to heed his wisdom, but instead I rushed headlong in the other direction.

Chapter Ten

"YOU MUST BE BLAKE'S FATHER!"

Shortly after Scott's death, my father took a decade-long sabbatical from me and mine. Most of this had to do with my spectacular lack of rapport with Sandra and her kids, which came to a head during my father's seventieth birthday celebration at Breeze Hill, where Sandra billeted my wife, seven-week-old daughter, and me in a room containing the only public toilet for all the other weekend guests, who drunkenly banged in and out all night while our sleep-deprived baby wailed and writhed. (My stepsister and her family stayed in the luxurious guest wing and were unwilling to swap after that first awful night.) Subsequently I wrote our hosts a grand remonstrance, tabulating this grievance and various others, to which Sandra replied in kind. Hence the almost ten-year silence that ensued.

Around September 2013, however, Burck seemed to have caught wind of my imminent memoir about our fucked-up family, *The Splendid Things We Planned*, or so I surmised when I Googled an online press-release announcing the Burck and Sandra Bailey Scholarship in Law for the Benefit of Native American, African American, and Hispanic Students at the University of New Mexico (because they now lived in Santa Fe). To some extent, I daresay, this was meant as a preemptive PR strike in the face of what Burck and Sandra surely expected would be my withering portrayal of their manifold failings as parents and human beings. Endowing that scholarship had doubtless cost them a pretty penny, but it would certainly burnish their image and besides they wouldn't be needing that dosh as a bequest for me or any of my descendants.

I'd just stepped into the elevator of my New York hotel, going down, en route to a reading from *Splendid* at McNally Jackson bookstore in SoHo, when I got a call from my mother.

"Guess who I just heard from?" she asked in a giddy voice.

". . . Sandra?"

"How'd you know?"

An educated guess. Once she'd gotten over her initial revulsion toward my mother, Sandra would often affect a great open-minded fondness for her ("We love Marlies!"), perhaps on the principle that one should keep one's friends close but one's enemies closer. Sandra had especially liked to remind *me* that she loved Marlies, no doubt in penance for her earlier (and current, truth be known) hard feelings toward us both. At other times, though, she'd betray something less than love for Marlies, especially after some fresh boorishness on the latter's part: "Really, Blake," she'd sigh at such times, "Burck and I just wish she'd go away." As for Marlies's attitude toward Sandra (never mind Burck), it was every bit as ambivalent as vice versa, though Marlies was more at ease with her own mixed feelings. She gave Sandra credit for making Burck happy, after all, and recognized on some level that Sandra's efforts to be friends with her were all the more heroic for being, at bottom, utterly disingenuous.

"Your glee could only mean Sandra," I said. "Let me guess: she read my memoir?"

My mother cackled: "'How do you feel about your *"dysfunctional"* family, Marlies?'"

"So, wait, Sandra's saying our family *wasn't* dysfunctional—?"

"She thought I'd be just as pissed off as she is. She wanted to commiserate. I told her I thought the book was *great* . . ."

Good old Marlies. By then she'd all but forgotten the invidious early chapters—where I'd portrayed her as the tipsy, deracinated Emma Bovary of the Okie boondocks—and glommed on to the later bits about her valiant if misguided attempts to save Scott from his certain doom. But probably she would have been loyal to me in any case, at least vis-à-vis Sandra, who seemed piqued by Marlies's lack of indignation and mumbled something evasive when the latter proposed they catch up over lunch. (They never spoke again.)

So Sandra was not a fan of my book. Burck, however, had reason to be pleasantly surprised: there were a few shy-making references to his rutting with the twenty-three-year-old Mandy, but mostly I'd been nothing but charitable in portraying him as he was at his best, and in my Acknowledgments I commended his "sweetness and decency." After he died, his copy of *Splendid* came into my hands, and I noticed he'd made little checkmarks in the margins throughout—next to passages (I assume) that he'd deemed potentially actionable, or wanted to revisit for whatever reason, and a whole asterisk bloomed next to this paragraph:

> . . . whatever her niceness otherwise, Sandra said terrible things behind my back to whosoever would listen—her children, friends, neighbors, Burck's law partners, even our longtime maid, Katherine Jones, who doted on me and couldn't understand why I was determined to cross a nice person like Sandra, who in her best Lady Bountiful fashion had taken her to see *The Color Purple*. Quite simply I combined everything Sandra disliked in a human being, and was a rival for her husband's affection besides.

So, again, Sandra had less reason to be pleased, but whatever qualms Burck himself entertained were mitigated, I think, by an email he received from Don Lamm, the emeritus president and chairman of W. W. Norton, my new publisher. Don had obtained an early copy of *Splendid* from his successor, Drake McFeely, and was almost certainly the one who'd alerted Burck and Sandra to my book in the first place. Don had also retired to Santa Fe, where he and Burck were members of the same high-powered book club. Commending Burck as "a man of utmost integrity," the kindly Don wrote of my memoir:

> . . . By any measure, it is a searing account that any parent could say, "there but for the grace of God . . ." It speaks to your steadiness under extreme stress all the while leading a distinguished career.
>
> In great admiration. . . .
>
> PS. If Blake is in town one time [Don may have wondered why he'd never seen me there], I'd like to shake his hand. Not only is he a fine writer, he displayed true grit in writing the book.

My estrangement from Burck had encompassed the first decade of my daughter's life, and we agreed that his peacemaking visit (sans Sandra) to our home in Virginia should coincide with my daughter's end-of-the year festival at the Burton School. Prior to his arrival on June 5, 2014, Burck paved the way by mailing me a couple of DVDs and an old VHS tape. One DVD was a clamorously dramatic (heavy metal soundtrack, jagged editing) video of his parachuting from an airplane on his seventy-fourth birthday—a bucket-list item from his "adventurous life" (obituary), whose items also included a climb to the 20,000-foot summit of Mount Kilimanjaro at age sixty (we'd been estranged then too). The other DVD was a long recent interview with his friend Ralph Thompson for the Historical Society of the Western District of Oklahoma—a quintessential performance of the public Burck, that witty, self-deprecating raconteur, a perfect companion for a rainy night before a cozy fire. And lest I think it was all about reminding me of his best self, the old VHS tape was a bizarre curio: Scott's audition for the Music Department at Oklahoma City University, circa 1995—what would have been his third foray, age thirty-four, into higher education—just before the head injury he sustained in his last, most spectacular car wreck, which effectively ended any hope of his ever contributing to

society and hence the six years he spent in prison toward
the end of his life. Amid the bleeding, blurry colors of
old VHS, Scott marches stiffly into the frame dressed in
a cheap suit he bought for the occasion, puffs his chest,
and sings "Some Enchanted Evening"—a so-so Ezio Pinza
imitation he doubtless practiced in the shower.

The actual Burck looked small standing with his suitcase
outside the baggage claim at Norfolk airport, glancing
around in a somberly cautious way. I popped out of my
car, gave him a big hug, and said something about how
wonderful he looked (versus how frail he felt).

He eyed me a little doubtfully and tried to smile: "Well,
son, you don't look *too* bad yourself . . ." (emphasizing *too*,
as in not so great).

During the half-hour drive to Portsmouth in rush-
hour traffic, he seemed almost sheepish with fatigue: the
flight from Albuquerque, with a layover somewhere, had
taken nine or ten hours, and that was a lot for an emaciated almost-eighty-year-old man. His voice had an elderly
quaver.

"They're brats," he murmured, when I asked him about
my stepsister Kelli's daughters, Beau and Belle. "I think
Kelli believes it's 'bourgeois' to discipline them."

It was the nastiest thing he'd ever said (or ever would
say) about his stepdaughter, and I suppose he was permit-
ting himself to be candid in order to make things go.

My own shy daughter was a little nervous about meeting
her mysterious grandfather for the first time, and I hoped
she wouldn't do or say anything to make Burck quietly
assess her as a brat—but au contraire: She and my wife

were waiting by the front door, and the change in Burck was wonderful to see. In a flash all his weary gruffness vanished; he gave my daughter his sweetest smile—one of the sweetest smiles to be found anywhere on earth, I was reminded—and she lit up in kind.

We took Burck to the nicest restaurant in those parts, Stove, and he held forth about his post-retirement teaching junket in Romania and the like. I'd gone from thinking he was a wizened, sadly diminished specter of his former self to wondering whether he was aging in reverse, and realized how much of his subdued manner during our drive from the airport was due to simple discomfort, after all these years, in my company.

After Burck had kissed my wife and daughter good night, he and I stayed up tippling and chatting. Before his visit I'd asked him whether there was anything special I should have on hand during his stay, and he'd requested a large bottle of Bombay Sapphire gin. One martini made him volubly charming, but he went on to have several and reverted to a vitiated specter toward the end. He'd just told me, in a thick slurring murmur—I had to lean forward to catch his words—about the second or third time he'd gone to New York to save my crazy brother, i.e., the time Scott wasn't allowed on the plane because he was vividly impaired and insisted, at the last moment, on bringing a mangy cat aboard. In the silence that followed this grim tale, I noticed my father's head begin to nod and suggested we call it a night. On the stairs his legs went out on him, and I caught him from behind and more or less carried him up to the guest bedroom. By then he weighed maybe

125 pounds, and I thought of my mother's gleeful refrain about his looking like a Buchenwald survivor.

THE NEXT MORNING I thought of Cheever, circa 1961, just after he'd moved into his fine old Dutch Colonial stone-ended house in Ossining and invited his elderly friend Josie Herbst to stay for the night. Herbst had drunk too much and slept ominously late the next morning, while Cheever worried about tapping on her door and finding her dead. Burck had always been an early riser, and I had similar misgivings as I remembered his limp body on the stairs the night before, but I found him drowsily smiling when he bade me enter.

The Burton School was a couple of ramshackle mansions opposite each other in the Ghent neighborhood of Norfolk. It was more arty and progressive than most private schools in the area, and the families at the end-of-the-year festival were all nice, well-educated folks. I was pleased to show Burck the whole genteel ethos and likewise pleased for our acquaintances to meet my charming, distinguished father (always at his best with strangers). My wife was kind to Burck and attentive about shepherding him around when I was detained with this or that person, but in truth she took a dim view of his ten-year desertion and had spoken of it freely with some of her friends, one of whom—the mother of our daughter's best pal—approached Burck and me just as we were settling into our chairs to hear the headmaster's opening remarks.

"You must be Blake's father!" she said brightly. "We've

waited *so* long to meet you! Blake's our celebrity, you know. We're so proud of him . . ."

This was laying it on pretty thick, and despite the treacle Burck knew when he was being chided. "Well, I should hope so!" he said heartily, but didn't get up or otherwise prolong the exchange.

THE NEXT DAY we took him to the Chrysler Museum, two or three gracious blocks away from our daughter's school. Like his son, Burck preferred to be left on his own in museums, so our wanderings diverged and in due course we were ready to leave and went looking for Burck. The Chrysler is rather large and labyrinthine, and after fifteen minutes or so I became a little worried. I'd checked every floor, every men's bathroom (peeking under the stall doors), but nothing.

"Maybe he's lost?" I murmured to my wife. By then we'd both noticed that Burck, for all his social poise, was apt to repeat himself and sort of tune-out now and then. I hated to embarrass him, but finally I asked the concierge to put out a discreet APB for my elderly father, whom I pictured wandering outside with a dazed look. Maybe five minutes later a museum employee with a walkie-talkie descended the stairs with Burck trailing a little behind. He was smiling at us in a receptive "What next?" sort of way.

DURING HIS NEXT visit that fall—he'd recently turned eighty—he confided to me that his conjugal sex life was still quite active. We were sipping our five-o'-clock martinis in the living room, while my wife and daughter (neither of them gin drinkers) were out walking the dog.

"Wow, really?" I said, with sincere amazement. "Viagra, or . . . ?"

"*Stendra*," he said lovingly. "Works faster. Ten minutes and I'm—" He gave a tomcat growl and made a little pouncing motion.

I was reminded of a story Burck liked to tell about his beloved mentor, Lee Thompson, the courtly late father of his friend Ralph, the judge. By age ninety or so, Lee was bent double with osteoporosis, and Burck, thirty years his junior, would patiently walk alongside him as they made their glacial way through the halls of the First National Building. One time a good-looking young woman passed them in the opposite direction, and old Lee sprung bolt upright—for the first time in years and perhaps the last time ever—to cast a wistful gaze at her receding figure.

"*Still* . . . ?" said Burck.

Hobbling along, bent double again, old Lee just shook his head and said, "It never goes away."

What made it all the more amazing, in Burck's case, was that his libido functioned in spite of his heavy drinking. By then I'd learned that our two nights of drunkenness were hardly an aberration for the latter-day Burck, who soaked pretty much every night without fail. Among the twenty boxes of papers I inherited after his death were medical records listing "Alcohol dependence" as one of his autumnal conditions—all the more worrying given his lifelong gastrointestinal woes, nowadays complicated by precancerous lesions on his pancreas, for which he took enzymes whose efficacy (or lack thereof) could be assessed on the basis of his Buchenwaldian appearance. Usually, with me, he just had the one big martini and wine with dinner, and that was the daily consumption he reported to doctors. But one night he told me—in a casual way, as if he were noting something odd about the weather—that he simply couldn't sleep at night unless he constantly tippled bourbon and watched old Westerns (waking at two, pouring more bourbon; waking at four—etc.) in a separate bedroom so not to disturb Sandra. This on *top* of the big nightly martini and half bottle of wine (they subscribed to a wine club and had one of those pricey glassed-in cellars). Rather than foul our second-floor bathroom with his diarrhea (exacerbated by a bum pancreas), Burck took to staying at a bed and breakfast around the corner, run by a Trump-y old lesbian who adored him. At the start of one of his longer stays he bought a big bottle of Maker's Mark, and a week or so later I stopped by his room and saw the bottle had maybe an inch or two left. I was concerned, but I held my tongue: he was my father, a sexually active gentleman of eighty, and I figured it was just hard for him amid the nighttime *nada*, alone with his fear of death and whatever else preyed on his mind.

HE HADN'T BECOME any nicer about my writing career. When I once, diffidently, wondered aloud whether he was familiar with a certain aspect of my Cheever biography, he not only admitted he'd never so much as cracked it, but vehemently shook his head and said something about how distasteful he found the subject—not just Cheever but really my whole oeuvre, what with its emphasis on sexually conflicted alcoholics with some degree of mental illness (the non-alcoholic, decidedly hetero Roth was not yet amongst, though God knows he had his own problems). Rather than retort that Burck himself was no slouch in the alcoholism department, I shrugged and said something like, "Well, American writers of the first rank tend to be drinkers, and writing fiction is a weird occupation unless you have some pretty bad psychic injuries to work out." Burck made a face as though I'd cut a fart, and again shook his head impatiently: he didn't *like* such people, and that was that. Another time I showed him my website, and he asked about a linked video interview I'd given the *Times*. It was only three or four minutes long, so I showed it to him; Burck watched with a puzzled frown—it was edited in a sort of impressionistic way, cutting among more or less random quotes—and, when it was over, he shook his head and changed the subject.

Sometimes he discussed a book of his own that he purported to be working on—about a case he'd argued (successfully) before the United States Supreme Court on behalf of the Oklahoma City Police. I'd heard the gist many times, and Burck told it incomparably well, about how an officer had shot a man who'd allegedly reached for a weapon concealed in his boot, though no weapon was subsequently found. There were all sorts of interesting ambiguities and nice points of law, but he'd been talking about the case for almost twenty years and I never saw any finished prose (two or three of the twenty boxes I received after his death were crammed with related files and depositions). Given his indifference to my own work, I allowed myself to be a little pointed on the subject of how one might proceed with writing a book that one actually intends to finish:

"I try to get to my desk every day at the same time," I said in effect, "and don't allow myself to get up for lunch, or anything else, until I've gotten a certain amount of work done . . ." I went on about setting deadlines and the like, talking in a carefully neutral voice to avoid the appearance of gloating.

Burck shrugged: "Our cleaner, Rosa, comes once a week, and I try to get out of her way. I have a little cubicle at the courthouse library, and when I think she's done, I go home."

The message was that he was only messing around at this point, keeping himself occupied with something he liked to think about, and the subtext, perhaps, was that he'd already accomplished enough in this life, thanks, and didn't need advice from the peanut gallery.

SOMETHING TERRIBLE HAPPENED to me around Valentine's Day, 2018, when Burck announced he was coming for a ten-day visit. By then I'd begun the actual writing (post research) of my Roth book, and, except for the odd lunch and weekend outing, I really couldn't spare myself during regular working hours—especially in light of my Valentine's Day disaster: losing myself in work was the only way to cope with the horror of it all, and there was no question of discussing it with anyone other than a couple of very sympathetic friends.

While I drove us home from the airport, Burck admitted that things were not going well between him and Sandra—and no wonder, given that he was taking a ten-day vacation away from her, moreover to spend time with her estranged stepson and his family; it must have occurred to her, as it certainly occurred to me, that things were a lot easier between Burck and me now that she was no longer part of the package. I asked what was the matter, and he evasively repeated that she was being disagreeable without going into the why of it.

"It's a shame," he said. "We're not gonna live forever, after all."

Part of her problem—the only part Burck was inclined to mention—was that she'd suffered an insidious, barely detectable stroke at some point that made speaking more and more difficult. She was seeing a speech therapist, but it wasn't really working, and this made her understandably glum. Again I reflected that his ten-day vacation was unlikely to help, but I suppose he needed at least that much time away.

We got through it. My wife and daughter did their best to keep Burck occupied when I couldn't get away from my desk, and at night the martinis kept my private horrors at bay while we entertained him. The last night of that long visit I walked him back to his bed and breakfast. Saying goodbye on the corner, I produced an old photo I'd found in one of Marlies's albums—hardly a happy memory for my father, to wit, Family Therapy Night at the state-ordered rehab facility circa 1982: dressed in an elegant summer suit and Panama hat, my forty-eight-year-old father stands solemnly facing my brother, who looks very institutional with his buzz cut and baggy checked pants. The night ended disastrously (see *The Splendid Things We Planned*), but in the photo Burck's hand is laid tenderly on Scott's shoulder. Gauchely, no doubt, I'd found it a touching encapsulation of the relationship.

My father examined the photo, smiling unhappily, then handed it back. "I just can't go there," he said, and we kissed goodbye.

Chapter Eleven

VICTORIA

Around Valentine's Day, 2018, as #MeToo was booming (Philip Roth had three months to live), I'd received my first intimation of disaster. I was sitting at my desk with my cell phone pressed to my ear, on hold with somebody or something, when I got an incoming call from my editor at Norton, Matt Weiland.

"Hey Matt. I'm on hold. Is it important?"

"You've been accused of a crime."

Just like that. I ended my hold call and listened, aghast, while Matt explained the gist of a brief, pseudonymous email that had been sent to the president of Old Dominion University (where I'd been a visiting professor from 2010 to 2016), Jodi Kantor of the *New York Times*, and various higher-ups at Norton. In the spring of 2015, the emailer alleged, I'd had "nonconsensual anal sex" with her, and moreover there were two witnesses (which made me absurdly picture two people in folding chairs squeamishly observing a nonconsensual sex act). Since I'd only had the one extramarital encounter in the spring of 2015, I knew the witnesses in question were Dwight Garner, a daily book reviewer for the *Times*, and his wife, Cree LeFavour, and what they'd actually witnessed was, I should think, more extenuating than not.

The day before—April 14, 2015—I'd been in Philadelphia, where I'd given a talk to a Penn class taught by a fellow biographer, Paul Hendrickson (*Hemingway's Boat*). The next day Dwight picked me up on campus and drove me an hour and a half to his home in Frenchtown, New Jersey, a place rather fraught with literary history: across the river in Bucks County, Pennsylvania, was where Cheever's old friend Josie Herbst had held court for decades at her little farmhouse in Erwinna, while, in Frenchtown proper, James Agee had written parts of *Let Us Now Praise Famous Men* and palled around with Delmore Schwartz, who'd moved there as a refuge from city and academia, an era of the poet's life memorably evoked in *Humboldt's Gift*. And there I was, the guest of honor at a dinner party hosted by one of the wittiest, most incisive book critics in the country—a man I'd considered a friend, or at least a pleasant acquaintance, ever since a day in 2005 when he'd mailed me a copy of a Cheever-related letter that he'd turned up in his own research for an Agee biography. Dwight's cover note referred to my Yates biography as "That Book"—capital T, capital B—and soon he began assigning reviews to me for the *Times*. Prior to that day in Frenchtown, I'd met Dwight in person on exactly four occasions: for drinks at a Times Square bar in 2005, when he was still an editor for the *Book Review*; for drinks at a Midtown bar in 2009, shortly after he'd been promoted to a daily reviewer and was still working on his Agee bio (and seemed a bit chagrined about that); again in 2009 at the Texas Book Festival in Austin, where he chaired a panel I was on; and finally at a rarefied 2014 event in Oslo, no less, whither we'd flown on the same plane as Leslie Jamison, with whom we haggardly breakfasted at a harbor bistro while waiting for our hotel rooms to become available. "In the past D[wight] has been a little taciturn with me," I wrote in my journal on April 20, 2015, five days after that dinner party in Frenchtown, "as if the burden were on me to be the entertaining one. More animated this time."

The other guests that night included (1) a novelist friend of Dwight's, (2) a woman whose name I thought was Victoria who turned out to be Cree's best friend, and (3) Chip McGrath, the former editor of the *New York Times Book Review*, whom I'd met six years before, when he came to my house in Virginia to interview me for a *Times Magazine* piece about Cheever. A memorable day. One of Chip's golfing buddies (along with my agent) was none other than John Updike, who, Chip revealed that day, was dying of lung cancer.* We were sitting in my living room—we'd finished the formal interview, gone to lunch, and were wrapping things up— when Chip told a funny story about how Updike had once inquired about the square-footage of Philip Roth's house in

---

* The last thing Updike finished for publication was a mixed review of my Cheever biography, which appeared in the *New Yorker* almost a month to the day after Updike's death on January 27, 2009. This may, in the end, prove my main (non-scandalous) claim to fame.

Connecticut. While I was laughing at this, Chip's cell phone rang—the *New York Times*. Updike had just died, sooner than expected, and Chip needed to drop everything and touch up a rather sloppy (I gathered) obituary drafted years ago by Christopher Lehmann-Haupt. Hastily I drove him to the airport, where the Wi-Fi was better. Six years later, in Frenchtown, I was glad to see Chip again, though my only vivid memory of him that night was the bored/weary look on his face while I tipsily sang a Sinatra tune at a karaoke bar we visited after dinner.

According to my journal, the other guests went home around midnight, whereas I and the woman whose name I thought was Victoria were spending the night chez Dwight and Cree. Dwight went to bed, but Cree suggested we stalwarts have another drink and watch *Lost in Translation*, a movie we all liked. She may or may not have wanted to give Victoria and me a chance to be together a bit longer and deepen our flirtation: I remember a long tipsy chat with Victoria earlier that evening, off in a corner, that apparently included a bit of canoodling—or so a mutual acquaintance reported Dwight's version of events, later, when the latter was gossiping about things at a cocktail party; I don't quite remember the earlier canoodling, but it seems plausible. Anyway the three of us sat on the sofa—Victoria, me, Cree, in that order—and "V. nuzzled close" (journal) in a way that struck me as unmistakably inviting, gradually leading to an emulation of Updike from a story he tells on himself in *Self-Consciousness*: while his first wife, Mary, drove them all home from the ski basin, Updike sat in the backseat masturbating one of her friends. In my case, vis-à-vis Victoria, this went on for half an hour or so, while Cree "sat on the other side [of me] affecting oblivion" (journal). Finally the movie ended, and the two women went to bed—Victoria to her assigned sofa in Cree's office on the top floor. I vaguely recall taking my time in the bathroom downstairs, then sitting or lying on my own assigned sofa bed wondering whether I should go upstairs and continue what had begun during the movie. I was tired and should have stayed put, but instead I went upstairs. One of my two or three worst decisions in a lifetime full of bad decisions.

In my journal I wrote about my exchange with Victoria as to whether it was safe to proceed without a condom. I was mostly out of the adultery business by 2015, except for a married woman—more of a pal, really—who lived far away and always conscientiously visited "the sin doctor" before one of our semi-annual (or so) trysts. As for Victoria, she said ("a little dispiritedly") "Can't remember the last time I had sex"—to that effect—so we thought it more or less safe to proceed. My journal reminds me that I dozed off for two or three hours afterward. What Victoria would later characterize as a criminal act was our second coupling that night—on my part, a groggy halfhearted attempt at middle-of-the-night missionary sex—what happens when you find yourself, still half-asleep, next to a naked body and do what comes naturally with a naked body. In my journal I wrote that she was "dry" that second time, a detail I wouldn't be able to summon now, at the distance of almost eight years, though I generally remember it wasn't pleasurable for either of us—certainly not for her, if she was dry for the reason I now assume (given what followed)—so I noticed the time

(4:30 a.m. or thereabouts) and suggested we try to get a bit more sleep. I rose to fetch us both glasses of water before retiring to my assigned sofa bed downstairs, whereupon Victoria farted and burst out laughing.

The next morning she sat on the edge of my sofa bed and we drank our coffee and chatted with our hosts. Everybody was a little hungover, but it was cheerful enough. I was at pains to be friendly to Victoria without, however, calling her by her first name, in case it turned out to be something other than Victoria. Finally Dwight drove me to the Philadelphia train station; I tried to be conversational but he was his old taciturn self by then, doubtless thinking about the latest review he had to write, or perhaps his Agee book, still on the rankling back burner. "That was big fun, man, thanks again for coming," he emailed me the next day. "(Pun not intended . . . but now that it's there, what the hey.)"

As I would learn six years later via the *New York Times*—wherein Dwight professed to be "horrified" by what had allegedly transpired that night—the woman's name was *not* Victoria, but rather something else starting with V and reminiscent of that bitter holiday when she'd written her pseudonymous email three years earlier. And yes, I'd worried about my decision not to contact her after the Garner dinner party: "The above encounter," I noted in my journal on April 24, 2015, four days after my previous "Victoria" entry, "continues to nibble at the edge of consciousness and give me an all but constant sense of impending doom." Call it Cad's Intuition. The fact is, I would have sent her at least some cordial note—hoping we meet again, inviting her to keep in touch, whatever—but I didn't have her contact info and hesitated to ask Cree or Dwight, lest I seem an even bigger cad/schmuck if, as it happened, I had gotten her name wrong. So I hoped she wouldn't be too affronted about things—that is, about this biographer of Philip Roth (a reputed philandering misogynist) who'd conspicuously tri-fled with her at the home of her rather famous best friends, then couldn't be bothered to write so much as a lousy email. I was pretty sure she knew I was married, after all, and per-haps she would simply figure I'd sobered up and decided not to complicate my life, and of course she was free to reach the same conclusion about her own life. But no.

Be that as it may. Circa Valentine's Day, 2018, I assured my editor at Norton that the accusation was unambiguously false and persuaded him to let me handle it. The email I sent to my accuser's pseudonymous account would eventu-ally be quoted in the *New York Times*: "My publisher for-warded your note. I can assure you that I have never had nonconsensual sex of any kind, with anybody, ever, and if it comes to a point I shall vigorously defend my reputation and livelihood. Meanwhile I appeal to your decency: I have a wife and young daughter who adore and depend on me, and such an accusation, even untrue, would destroy them."

As an unnamed literary agent would tell Andrew Anthony of *The Guardian* three years later, "Norton made a big mis-take there. They should have written back [to my accuser] in the first instance, clearly stating that it was a criminal matter which needed to be investigated by the appropriate authori-ties." Also, of course, Norton might have spared themselves a lot of expense/controversy if they'd endeavored to cancel my book *before* publication (as Hachette, say, had done with

Woody Allen's memoir) rather than *after*—but declined to do so, perhaps because (1) my book was *sui generis* (the only authorized biography written with the full cooperation of its famously private, soon-to-be-dead subject), and (2) there was no "morality clause"—standard for publishing contracts in the #MeToo era—in my own contract, signed in 2012, and Norton would have been on shaky legal ground (as indeed they were later).

As for the email I wrote to my pseudonymous accuser: someone would let me know, in 2021, when she first read it in the *Times*, that she found it "sickening" how I'd invoked my wife and daughter by way of covering my ass, and another friend (also female) described the whole note as "wormy," what with my use of the word *adore*, etc. I can only say in my defense that "adore" was the *mot juste*—I adored my wife and daughter and they adored me, and the last thing I wanted was to expose them to ruin with my rotten, reckless conduct, and I wanted my accuser to feel something of my urgency on that point. One of my friends ("wormy") conjectured, however, that my email almost certainly had the opposite effect than what I'd intended.

Chapter Twelve

FUNERAL FOR A FRIEND

On May 22, 2018—three months after Victoria's pseud-onymous email to the *Times*, ODU, and Norton—I dropped my bag at my friend Christopher's apartment in the West Village and headed uptown to New York Presbyterian, where I arrived around 5:30, or about five hours before Philip Roth's death. I knew he'd already received terminal sedation, and, according to a mutual friend, was not seeing visitors anymore. When I arrived, however, people roamed freely between the Cardiac ICU waiting room and the bed where Philip lay drawing his raspy, eruptive last breaths (quite like he'd described his father in *Patrimony*: "Dying is work and he was a worker"). If he'd had a spouse or children or any immediate family, they'd be the only ones allowed to pass; instead there were old friends and lovers and even a former employee.

I'd been there a few hours and was mustering my nerve to say a final goodbye, when an old lady, sitting behind me, said "Hello, Blake." I turned and smiled at her, racking my brain, and she reminded me—"Ann" . . . Mudge: Roth's long-ago love, a little older even than he; I hadn't seen her in almost six years, since we'd had our last interview (of three) in her winsomely cluttered Park Avenue apartment. We both looked older, and, briefly holding hands, we silently acknowledged as much.

It was around nine o' clock when I stood gazing at Philip for the last time. I can't say I ever felt a filial bond with him (though he and Burck were roughly the same age), nor were we like any biographer-subject I could think of. Still, I felt the honor and pleasure of our curious attachment, and at that moment I wanted to buss him on the forehead—were it not for the eminent historian Sean Wilentz keeping solemn vigil in the only available chair. So instead I gave his shoulder a light but fervent squeeze and thought something like: *Don't worry, Philip, it'll all come out in the wash.*

I WAS BACK at Christopher's apartment in the Village (which I had to myself; he and his wife lived elsewhere most of the year) when a friend phoned me from the hospital: Philip was dead. Somebody had already alerted the *Times*, and I did my part by finding a fifty-year-old photo of Philip on my laptop—one where he's looking young and sensitive versus grim and full-of-himself, as he almost invariably did in his latter-day portraits—and tweeting it along with the caption: "Philip Roth died tonight, surrounded by lifelong friends who loved him dearly. A darling man and our greatest living novelist." Immediately my phone exploded: not simply with the expected likes and retweets and whatnot, but with interview requests from all over the world. Roth, again, had no surviving family other than a few cousins he hardly knew, and since he'd always kept mum about his private life, the media had very little notion of who his friends were. That left me, his biographer.

The next day was a blur. My first interview around 5:30 a.m. was a phoner with NPR's Steve Inskeep, who wanted to know, among other things, whether Roth was "just writing about himself" given his many Roth-like alter egos. I heard myself describe this as "a terrible misconception" and gave as my first instance the way *Portnoy* readers had largely perceived the author as a "compulsive masturbator" and "antic sex fiend"—this while it quietly occurred to me that such a characterization was hardly wide of the mark—so I mentioned, too, how Zuckerman's father, on his deathbed, had cursed his son for writing *Carnovsky*, whereas Herman Roth was forever handing out copies of *Portnoy* inscribed "From Philip Roth's father, Herman." Afterward I was hoping to snatch an hour or two of sleep, but NPR called me back: there was some technical glitch with my last answer, so I waited for Inskeep to finish another interview and come back on the line and ask me again what Roth had thought of Donald Trump, whereupon I duly repeated Roth's anathemas on the subject. By then I had just enough time to squeeze in a quick shower before my Skype interview with the CBC.

Though *very* tired, I made it through that first day without quite embarrassing myself. Chip McGrath's front-page above-the-fold *Times* obit was already printed, but I was asked by a copy-person to look it over and let them know whether there were any factual errors (I found three very minor ones) so they could issue a timely online correction. Camera crews came and went through my friend's lovely but very small apartment: BBC, Agence France-Presse, the big German service (Deutsche Welle?), one or two others. They were in a hurry and didn't bother with soft lighting or makeup; later I looked up these interviews online and found the odd clip or still of myself looking like the Devil Himself (if the Devil were aging badly). It was dark outside by the time I wrapped up the ninth or tenth interview, and I walked a few blocks to Café Cluny, where I spent a couple hours at the bar swilling martinis and savoring a burger and fries—easily the high point of that day and the days to follow.

ROTH'S MOURNERS, a diverse group of eighty or so, boarded buses outside Riverside Chapel for the two-hour drive to Annandale-on-Hudson. I sat with an old lover/friend of Roth who'd become a friend of mine, Barbara Jakobson, and we had a nice desultory chat when I wasn't staring haggardly out the window. In my biography I describe the scene in the sun-dappled woods of Bard Cemetery; what I didn't say is how awkward I felt as the only authorized biographer of the deceased. In the *New Yorker,* David Remnick would write about spotting me there and wondering what

I was making of things; indeed, I found myself briefly tri-angulated with him and Janis Bellow, and couldn't think of a single thing to say. (A few months later Remnick and I chattered like schoolgirls on a Roth-themed episode of *The New Yorker Radio Hour*.) A muscular young Orthodox Jew with side curls, some kind of IT guy, buttonholed me for ten minutes or so, sharing a few stories about how he'd helped Roth navigate the technological puzzlements of the twenty-first century. He clearly wanted at least a cameo in my book, and I hated to disappoint him but disappoint him I would. And finally I betrayed my goyish fecklessness when I bungled the one traditional Jewish aspect of the funeral: namely, when it came time for each of us to drop a spadeful of dirt into Philip's grave. For my part I continued to shovel away with yeoman-like zeal (as we'd been expected to do at the recent funeral of my wife's grandfather, an Episcopalian priest), until another guest tapped me on the shoulder and silently asked to be given her turn.

Chapter Thirteen

CREEP

Mya was the youngest of the former students I'd slept with circa 2004. She was a small, pretty, olive-skinned girl with a minor disability I'd found poignant, all the more given her spunky way of dealing with it. She was sexually active at an early age and eventually told me all about it: her father had once caught her with a boy; she'd cheated on her main boyfriend with his best friend ("the worst thing I've ever done"). By the time she was sixteen, these confessions had become more lurid and pointed. In one of her emails she mentioned a "friend" who was very close to one of her male teachers, and each wanted to sleep with the other: What did I think of that? I was appalled (I was!) and said so. Next she told me about a family wedding that she—Mya herself, not a "friend"—had attended on the beach, which culminated in her slipping away with a male guest, who'd seduced her in the dunes. "Only problem," came the punch-line: "He's forty-four years old." (I was thirty-nine at the time.)

So anyway, reader, I slept with Mya (twice) when she was seventeen, and fifteen years later—in early 2019—she contacted my wife via social media and told her all about it.

"This is over," my wife told me. "I want you out of here today. Look for a furnished apartment somewhere . . ."

After a terrible discussion—mostly revolving around our daughter and her needs—we finally decided that I could stick around, for now, but would have to get intensive psy-chotherapy. And one thing was perfectly clear: a subject like Philip Roth was a lightning rod, especially in these times, and, as Mya had mentioned to my wife, she wasn't the only one who knew about my bad behavior; if anyone spoke to reporters, once my book came out, I would leave home immediately and draw the fire elsewhere, simple as that. (I should add that my wife still knew nothing about Victoria, my previous, pseudonymous accuser.)

DR. STERNBLATT WAS a yarmulke-wearing Orthodox Jew in his early seventies. He'd gone to an Ivy League college at a time when Jews were sparse in the Ivy League, and sometimes he'd reminisce when I'd mention, say, that Philip Roth and his friend Mel Tumin had been among the very few Jews teaching at Princeton in the sixties. Dr. Sternblatt knew who Roth was, of course, but his interests weren't literary, and, in any case, he wasn't terribly impressed by my credential as Roth's biographer—or rather he took quiet pains to let me know it was beside the point. When I'd bring up something like that, he'd maybe arch his eyebrows and wait for me to finish. Often, too, especially during those early sessions while we discussed my curious childhood, I'd mention *The Splendid Things We Planned*: "Of course this is all in my memoir . . ." To this day I don't know whether Sternblatt ever read it or not; he refused to say (though I read a book of his). Among his first assignments for me was to write an unmailed letter to my mother, and, while reading this aloud to him, I'd pause every so often and say "I tell it better in my book . . ."

He touched on such moments when it came time, at last, to lay his cards on the table somewhat.

"I notice you don't just say 'When I taught at ODU,' or 'When I was a professor at ODU'; you say 'When I was Darden Chair at ODU . . .'"

"I thought I was just being specific." (This a little tongue-in-cheek perhaps.)

"Well, I think it has something to do with those girls of yours . . ."

"Really? How so?"

"I think it would be more"—he used a term like *clinically* or *therapeutically efficacious*, but something else—"if you told me yourself."

"Oh. I see. You're saying I'm a narcissist."

I seem to recall he mildly deplored the word as reductive, while allowing that, yeah, that was pretty much the gist of it.

"But don't you think maybe the opposite is also a little true?" I pursued. "That on some level I kind of *despise* myself? I mean, it's occurred to me that all this behavior is by way of destroying whatever happiness I've ever managed to achieve . . ."

Well, he said, but that's part of it. You have the wound, and the wound is gaping: this insatiable need for love and approval . . .

"Reading the psychoanalyst Karen Horney one night," I'd written about Cheever on page 207 of my biography, "he realized that he was 'implicated in the neurotic picture,' given his insatiable need for love and approval (often caused by 'parental indifference,' said Horney) . . . he strained himself to write kindly, witty, intimate letters to almost total strangers; his public persona was unassailably charming (belied withal by the depressive paranoia of his journal); he followed comely people around on the street; he felt an 'erotic, childish' hankering almost all the time . . . But why speak only of the neurotic's 'frustrations,' he wondered, when 'a good deal of poetry and charm can be involved'?"

It was an aspect of Cheever's brilliance that he took his bleak epiphany and turned it into one of his greatest stories, "The Country Husband," about a non-poetic Everyman named Francis Weed (lest we miss the point): "He had not developed his memory as a sentimental faculty. Wood smoke, lilac, and other such perfumes did not stir him, and his memory was something like his appendix—a vestigial repository." Weed is roused from his quotidian slumber when he survives a plane crash and then, the next day, is unexpectedly reminded of the war in all its arch reality. His senses "dilated," he becomes preternaturally aware of the world's beauty and sensual promise: at the train station he sees a naked blond woman sitting in her compartment combing and combing her hair; he tells old Mrs. Wrightson, a local busybody who intrudes on his happiness, to shut up; and finally—most notably, of course—he falls in love with his seventeen-year-old babysitter, which leads to his tearfully seeing a shrink ("I'm in love, Dr. Herzog").

The subjects of my biographies are beset by various psychological afflictions—addiction of one sort or another; psychotic bouts of mania in Yates's case—though perhaps the most common thread is their narcissism, at least if you believe their shrinks: "There's your narcissism again!" Dr. Kleinschmidt liked to remind Philip Roth; "I don't think I've ever known anybody else in my life who needs love as badly as you do," Dr. Anthonisen told Charles Jackson; "His major personality trait is his narcissism," Dr. Silverberg (and others, invariably) noted of Cheever, "and underneath it all is tremendous self-doubt."

Mostly I relate to their loneliness: the way they mitigate the shame of their behavior by idealizing the most improbable love objects—Cheever and his Mormon, Max Zimmer; Jackson and his Czechoslovakian laborer, Stanley Zednik; Roth and, well, don't get me started. Zimmer was flummoxed by the elaborate lengths to which Cheever would woo him—the daily letters full of complicated irony, lacerating expressions of love and guilt, etc. ("God, how'm I gonna answer these letters?" Max remembered thinking. "I'm just a hick from Utah.") When I mentioned to Mya, in 2004, that I was working on a proposal for a biography of Cheever—one of whose greatest stories was about a middle-aged man's infatuation with his seventeen-year-old babysitter—Mya read "The Country Husband" and replied, in so many words, "I don't recall *you* saying anything about being in love." Whereupon I was quite smitten for a few months; whereupon we both took to signing our emails with "love" and sometimes "love love." Later she would claim that I'd pushed her to read *Lolita*—but no, not exactly: I quite agree with Nabokov's own assessment of Humbert as "a vain and cruel wretch who manages to appear 'touching,'" and I don't remotely regard the novel as a Baedeker for intergenerational love; vis-à-vis Mya, though, I couldn't resist a droll reference or two (likening Lolita's "brown fragrance" to hers, say), and Mya would later remember this as my using the book as a wooing tool.*

During that bewildering spring of 2004, I mentioned Mya to an old friend in New York, a worldly woman in publishing, and also mentioned a few other unseemly dalliances.

"But the seventeen-year-old seems special."

"She is." She was at the time.

My friend spared me the worst of her consternation, but

---

* The *Times-Picayune* reported on April 20, 2021, that I assigned *Lolita* to my eighth-graders. Had I not been almost catatonic at the time, I would have laughed. Whenever I assigned a "challenging" book like *Slaughterhouse-Five*, I'd send a letter home to parents explaining my reasons for doing so and warning them as to content; they could either sign-off on the book in question or request an alternative assignment. That would have been an interesting letter in the case of *Lolita*. The only reference to *Lolita* in any of my eighth-grade classes was during the course of a yearly one-day lesson on Good Writing, wherein I explained Somerset Maugham's tripartite criteria—Lucidity, Simplicity, and Euphony, in that order—and discussed these in terms of nine exemplary prose passages on a hand-out. One of the passages was the opening lines of *Lolita* ("Lolita, light of my life . . ."), which I consider an all but perfect synthesis of the three criteria. "And perhaps our greatest prose stylist," I said once a year for seven years, "spoke English as a second language!"

was stern on one point: "Blake, she thinks she's the only one. For your sake, I hope she never finds out otherwise."

SUCH WERE THE friends who were simply fond of me and remain enduringly puzzled and/or depressed by my behavior in those days. For the *Slate* piece, "Mr. Bailey's Class," my former student Mary Laura N. forbore to invoke a *Lolita*-like canard about my teaching practices or affect to be shocked by my occasional ribaldry. She remembered writing in her journal that she wanted to be a flight attendant, to which I'd facetiously replied that it was a job that "lent itself to promiscuity": "Nobody wants to hear that thirteen-year-olds are sexual beings," Mary Laura commented for *Slate*, "but they are coming into their sexuality. So those off-color comments just made us feel more seen, and more respected."

Mary Laura's account of our friendship over the years is perfectly accurate: we met for coffee now and then; once or twice I had dinner at her parents' house. After college she moved to New York, and in the midst of my 2004 derangement I took her back to my hotel and tried to seduce her. We smooched a little but she made it clear there was nothing doing, and I remember her demeanor vividly: almost a kind of amusement, edged with concern, as in *Why are you* doing *this?* . . . Why indeed? I was fond of Mary Laura but, truth be known, didn't much want to sleep with her any more than vice versa. And the world was my oyster! I'd miraculously sprung the lock on my terrible teaching job in Gainesville (the one I'd gotten in a panicked hurry after Picador had passed on that third book proposal), and now was working on my Cheever biography for Knopf. I loved my wife and was so lucky to have her, never mind the precious daughter we'd be raising together: Why was I hurting them this way? Why? *Why?* Why was I betraying the trust and affection of everybody who'd ever cared about me? "He was such a good friend and teacher and we loved him so much," Mary Laura told *Slate*. "And totally trusted him. *Totally* trusted him. And I'm just going to put this out there: Still love him. Still."

But let me give the last word to Lori (I'll call her), who was anonymous in the *Slate* piece. I saw her verdict and knew it was her. I'd been dreading it for years. Lori thought she was unpretty and unlovable and viewed the world through the same harsh lens; where the world was concerned, at least, she was not inaccurate in her judgments. In her journal she always referred to her mom (a woman who reminded me in certain ways of Yates's mother and muse, Dookie) as "Bitch"; once, I pointed out that she'd accidentally written "Mom" here and there, and she promptly plied the white-out and substituted "Bitch." Another student of mine was a harmless, whimsical girl with a Chelsea haircut, and Lori wrote in her journal that the girl was a "turd." Not for the first time I admonished her meanness, while privately reflecting that "turd" was, though perhaps not the whole story, at least a part of it. Finally, like a lot of people who decide, for whatever reason, that they're unworthy of love, Lori had a Puritan aversion to sex—a sense (again: not inaccurate) that it had a lot to do with weakness and corruption. Through the years, I repeat, I wondered whether Lori knew the worst about me and what she would say if she did. Well then, without further ado, here's what the forty-year-old Lori said:

"Before him and after him, I never had a single teacher who gave two shits about me or thought I was interesting. The one guy who stood up for me, and he turned out to be a creep."

After my wife found out about Mya in February 2019, I was determined to save me and my family with sheer mulish labor—as I'd been trying to do, in any case, for years—flogging myself to write a book so good nobody or nothing could stop it.

Working practically every waking hour, seven days a week, I finished a draft of *Philip Roth* in June 2019; then, as we'd done for the past five years, my wife and I drove our daughter to camp in West Virginia, stopping along the way in little Shenandoah towns like Staunton (home of the American Shakespeare Theatre), Lexington, et al.—but this time, after dropping our daughter off, we went our separate ways for the duration of her absence.

On the Fourth of July—before heading to Williamstown, Mass., to visit a friend I'd made while working on my Charles Jackson book—I paid my final respects to whatever remained of Roth's ghost at his beloved old home in Litchfield County, Connecticut. His caretaker, Russ Murdock, had agreed to let me into the house so I could have a look around, but first I ate blueberry pancakes chez Murdock with Russ and his wife, Wendy. Russ is the kind of quirky, self-sufficient man's man whom Philip (and I) had always liked and rather envied perhaps. He'd built his impressive log house with his own hands and was an avid reader to boot. (I remembered Lillian Hellman's comment when a young Norman Mailer showed her the plumbing he'd installed in his Brooklyn apartment: "Norman, I admire you more for this than for *The Naked and the Dead*.") Wendy was a pleasant if taciturn woman who took care of illustrious horses (including a former Olympian) whose owners no longer wanted to keep them but didn't want to shoot them either. The pancakes were about the best I ever ate.

In Roth's novella *The Humbling*, when Simon Axler loses his magic and retires from acting, he reflects: "It's sometimes astonishing, sitting here month after month, season after season, to think that it's all going on without you. Just as it will when you die." The world went on without Philip Roth, but his eighteenth-century farmhouse looked bereft. Roth's favorite part of the house, the Stone Room—Chinese lantern orbs, *haimish* wicker furniture, glittering bars of sunlight from the big French doors—was shabby now: the rafters stunk of mold, and the only remaining furniture, Roth's beloved old refectory table, looked as though it were waiting for the dump. Most of Roth's possessions had already gone to auction, and now all that was left were his books (soon to be removed to the Philip Roth Reading Room at the Newark Public Library) and clothing (a few shirts were still tagged from the dry cleaners but frosted on the shoulders with mold). The plastic pool cover sagged with muddy stagnant water, buzzing with mosquitos. How swiftly nature had reclaimed the place, I thought, when Russ and I noticed a lone, corpulent porcupine ambling across the lawn. I tried to take a picture, but the porcupine gave me a gloomy fuck-off look and hastened away, wishing only to be left in peace.

Among his other talents, Russ is a stonemason and was sometimes called upon to repair the mossy, venerable walls on Roth's property. At Roth's request, Russ had found an old boulder to serve as Roth's gravestone, on which Russ had roughly carved (after the manner of Camus's gravestone) Roth's name and dates. What a mourner does not see is what Russ carved on the submerged concrete base: "At it again?"—Leopold Bloom's thought, in *Ulysses*, while masturbating at the sight of lovely (but lame) Gerty MacDowell.

A YEAR OR so before my world was destroyed, I dreamed about Philip. At the time I was struggling with depression, which I used to keep at bay, more or less, by burying myself in work—by thinking about Philip, in other words. But the book was mostly done, and he was gone. In the dream I was at a crowded gathering, with no one to talk to, feeling vaguely despised, when I spotted Philip wordlessly circulating. Only I seemed to notice him. He was dead (those eyes!) but oddly corporeal, and I flung myself into his arms— either I was child-sized or he was monolithic—and sobbed and sobbed. He briefly held me and let me cry, then put me down and shambled away, wishing only to be left in peace.

Chapter Fourteen

STICK A FORK IN ME

I can't ever discuss how the whole shit show affected my wife and daughter. I doubt I could find words even if I tried. Otherwise I mostly worried about Burck. The fate of his first-born son had been revealed in gruesome detail via *The Splendid Things We Planned*, with the unexpectedly happy result that he and I were a loving father and son again. And now, with my Roth book—for which the early buzz had been (though I say it myself) ecstatic—I seemed to be lifting the curse of Burck's first family and its many sorrows. Moreover he seemed to enjoy my success, at long last: in his March 27, 2021, email, he let me know how eager he was to watch my interview on *CBS Saturday Morning*—"I have recorded the slot, because (no surprise) I'm not up that early these days"—and was looking forward to reading the *New York Times Magazine* profile, etc.

But the subject-heading of this email—"thanatopsis"—suggested what was foremost on his mind:

> To quote Diana Athill, I'm somewhere towards the end—and not at all morbid about it. I've lived a very long life, with its stretches of rough road, but also a lot of clear sail. I don't have any life-threatening issues that I know of, so could be around for quite awhile. But my daily visit to the obits in *The Oklahoman* show me that only a few of my old legal colleagues and adversaries make it this long.
>
> I recently pre-paid for service-free cremation at Rivera funeral home here in Santa Fe. I thought I should let you know. I want my ashes given to Sandra, for her to do with them as she wishes. Most importantly, I most emphatically do not want any kind of funeral service. I think you know that as a teen-ager, I worked several summers (and, for awhile, after school) at The Burckhalter Funeral Home. Even at that young age, I was a bit appalled at the ghoulishness of many funeral services. I've watched many a troupe of folks gaze upon the embalmed remains as they dutifully pass by the open casket. Yikes. Not for me. . . .

At the time my father had a little less than eight months to live. When my life turned to shit, among the first things that occurred to me was a hopeless but fervent wish that Burck of all people might have been spared his son's spectacular public humiliation. If only he'd died, say, a week or two after *Philip Roth* was published, he would have quit this vale of tears thinking my life was a triumph, and meanwhile he would have shone all the brighter in the eyes of Don Lamm and suchlike peers—a great lawyer who'd sired a great literary biographer.

It was not to be.

Laura Marsh's review in the *New Republic* ("adoring wingman") and Parul Sehgal's in the *Times* ("sprawling apologia") had naturally been ballyhooed all over social media as proper feminist "takedowns" of Roth and me, until a notorious internet troll (male) got the idea to piggyback on such attacks by indignantly demanding an explanation of me, via Twitter, as to why I'd indulged in such a "misogynistic" portrayal of Roth's first wife, Maggie. Sidestepping the matter of the troll's own well-known misogyny, I could only assure him (pointlessly, since he knew exactly what he intended to say about me and Roth) that I'd done due diligence and then some—interviewing Maggie's first husband, two children, best friend, closest coworker, Roth himself, and also poring over her letters, journal, and odd scraps of abortive fiction. What I wrote was a faithful representation of these sources, and frankly I think Maggie comes across as a fascinating rogue—not very sympathetic, to be sure, but certainly three dimensional. The troll, however, was unpersuaded, and proceeded to post a copycat piece on his blog with "Misogynist" in the title—referring to me, not Roth—and for a few days this appeared as a primary hit if you Googled me. Among those who Googled, evidently, was a former Lusher student I'll call Rona, who posted a vicious comment on the troll's blog before seeking out a local reporter in New Orleans with four other long-ago students of mine, including Eve.

The better to distance himself from the troll's vitriol, my agent very publicly fired me the day after Rona's claim (in her blog comment) that I'd "assaulted" certain of my eighth-grade students. I'm omitting details I can't ever bear to relive, but suffice it to say I left home, as promised, to take a ruminative two-day drive to my best friend's apartment in Manhattan. I was still hoping it wouldn't be so bad, maybe, when I emerged from a drug store on the Eastern Shore of Virginia—where (as I recall) I bought facial moisturizer and gum—and checked my email in the car before getting back on the road. Sitting there in the parking lot, I saw that the Associated Press and *Los Angeles Times* and one or two others (with a multitude to come) wanted to know if I had any comment about the "very serious allegations" (my agent's words), whereas a longer email from the *Times-Picayune* minutely recounted the stories that my former students had told, which would be all over New Orleans (and presently the World) the next day. I skimmed these with dizzying horror.

"As you may already know," I wrote Burck three days later, "I am ruined." When Eve accused me of rape in the *Times-Picayune*—the day after Taffy Brodesser-Akner's feature in the *New York Times* surveying the tumultuous reception (good and bad) of my sensational book about Roth, her favorite author, whose best novels she enumerated and discussed at length—the *Times* promptly got back in touch with my 2018 accuser, Victoria (as I still thought of her), and persuaded her to doff the pseudonym and come forward with her own rape story. When W. W. Norton caught wind of these developments, they promptly announced they were "pausing" publication of *Philip Roth*, and the whole story blew up on the front page of the *Times*, which my father usually made a point of reading. In my email I explained to him how all this had come to pass, and how much of it was true—essentially that I'd stayed in touch with a number of my students over the years, and later had sex with a few of them. I told him what had actually happened with Eve and Victoria; I assured him I had a good lawyer, and my friends were being very kind, and so on, "But it's hell, and I'm not sure how I go on from here. I'm glad you're alive, but I hate that you've lived to see this happen. Know that I love you dearly, and I'm so unspeakably sorry that my reckless conduct has hurt you."

If Burck had cut me dead or responded with any kind of ambivalence at all—well, I won't say that I would have definitely killed myself, but it would have weighed in the balance. Instead, an hour or so later, he wrote: "I want you to know that I am here for you. Stay strong, be brave, aim high. Tomorrow will be different than today. Time will help. I love you. Papa."

The day after my arrival in Manhattan—April 20, 2021, when the *Times-Picayune* story broke—was the first day of the rest of my life as a reputed rapist. While on the Eastern Shore I'd stayed overnight at a little hotel in the town of Onancock (yes), where I lay on my bed tippling and reading Brodesser-Akner's nice-enough piece about Roth and me in the *Times*; when I woke up, a few hours later, my laptop was no longer working because I'd spilled a plastic cup of bourbon on the keyboard after passing out. So the first thing I did in New York was walk from my friend's apartment to the Apple Store in the Village, where I was informed that my laptop was a goner. I was waiting for my Genius to bring me a new one when I glanced at my phone and saw that I was blowing way the fuck up on Twitter. A person who'd written a long gushy blurb for my Roth book was losing no time repenting of her generosity, while her vast claque of followers egged her on, including a sometime writer friend of mine (male) who'd been one of my Zoom interviewers only a few days before, and now was tweeting about how utterly tainted he felt to have ever known me however remotely. I felt like a despised gladiator surveying a stadium of downward-jabbing thumbs while a lion gnashes at my ankle; before letting the lion finish his business, I wanted to sling my trident with all remaining strength in the direction of that opportunistic weasel of a so-called friend getting his nasty little digs in.

"You gotta cancel my Twitter account," I said to my friend Christopher, when I returned from the Apple Store a thousand-or-so dollars poorer. I think it was understood that I was incapable at that moment of just about anything but breathing. Christopher has a hand-tremor at the best of times, and I remember his palsied attempt to follow the prompts until finally my Twitter page vanished forever, and I no longer had to look at the little alerts popping up on my phone telling me again and again what a scumbag I was. And mind, this was still two days *before* the front-page story in the *Times* about Victoria, Norton's "pausing" my book, and so on.

Christopher had been the first person who saved my life. After my agent publicly fired me because of what was blowing up on the troll's website, and I had to leave home immediately, Christopher invited me to come to his apartment and stay as long as I liked. At the time I didn't know that I could be credibly accused of anything worse than lechery, and thought I'd make a soul-searching two-day holiday out of my drive from Portsmouth to Manhattan, stopping in Onancock that first night and Chincoteague (where I could rent a bicycle and pedal around the Assateague nature reserve) the second. Between Onancock and Chincoteague, however, fell the shadow—those dire emails from various media outlets—and I was beginning to think it might be best/easiest for all concerned if I just hanged myself that night in my Chincoteague hotel room. Meanwhile I was morbidly checking email again and again while driving, and would have almost certainly had a high-speed rear-end collision if I hadn't thought to call Christopher, who implored me to put away my phone, skip Chincoteague *for fuck's sake*, and come straight to his place in Manhattan, even though he and his wife were celebrating their anniversary at the Union Square Café that night and the Blakester would be a pretty lugubrious third wheel. I arrived in the Village a little before six and had to wait by my car until it was legal to park on the street; while I stood there talking with my distraught daughter on the phone, Christopher came trotting around the corner to give me a cup of cold gin.

My father had always taken wry pleasure in reciting Polonius's advice to Laertes, especially that bit about grappling friends ("their adoption tried") to one's soul with hoops of steel—a tenet that has stood me in good stead, my many shortcomings otherwise. When the world is howling for your blood, you learn in short order who your friends are. And, decidedly, who they aren't. Christopher held my hand through the worst of the news cycle—though he had pressing business at home in another state—until he was spelled by our friend William, the former newspaper editor who would later summarize the major articles about my depravity so I wouldn't have to read them word for word. Meanwhile I visited and was visited by various other friends in town. I have a wealthy old pal who divides his time between Oklahoma and the Upper East Side, and when I explained to him over dinner that I was about to be broke (I'd just paid my criminal [versus divorce] lawyer's retainer fee), he arranged an ingenious long-term job of ghostwriting on generous terms. Monica Yates emailed me two or three times a day during that first week or two, offering a lot of peppery perspective on things, while Susan and Ben

Cheever caught up with me over an improbably jolly dinner at a restaurant popular among literary nobs. The two managed to make me laugh even while I quietly wondered whether one of our fellow diners would dump a drink over my head. Earlier that day Barbara Jakobson had shared with me an email exchange (printed out for my records) between her and a celebrated person who was slagging me on Twitter. Wherefore such rabid animus, Barbara had inquired, especially given the slagger's one-time purported fondness for me and my book? Among other weird slanders in the slagger's reply, she claimed to have heard from "the friend of a *very good* friend" (my italics: not just the friend of a friend, in other words) that I'd anally raped a woman at a wedding. *Whose wedding?* I couldn't help wondering, before realizing—a little pensively—that I'd never even had conventional sex at a wedding, much less . . .

Most of my old friends were wonderful; in some cases, my scandal reunited me with beloved people who'd fallen out of touch. Shelly and I chatted for at least an hour, catching up on what had happened to each other since our paths diverged after my marriage and her divorce twenty-odd years before. "Oh Blake, did I *fail* you?" said sweet Jennifer, my closest female friend going back to childhood, who knew my raffish side better than most and had always tried to be a good influence. As it happened, I was also close friends with Jennifer's sister-in-law, a fellow writer; I knew she'd be getting an earful, so I promptly texted her that the worst of the allegations were distortions. Curtly she replied that, while she would always care for "my family," she needed time to think about things—fuck off, in short.

After that, I never again reached out to people, but rather let them decide whether they wanted to take the first step.

Indeed, the whole ordeal served as a baleful lesson on the, shall we say, utilitarian nature of most literary/professional friendships. Christopher and William are both writers themselves, and staunchly loving and loyal to me, but most of my other literary "friends" all but fell over one another (FIRE!) heading for the exits. Prior to my scandal I'd made plans with a writer pal to have one of our periodic lunches at Balthazar, right around the corner from her apartment in SoHo. She didn't cancel outright—what was happening was too juicy—but asked me to come under cloak of darkness, as it were, to her apartment. That was the day Eve's first-person rape story appeared in *Slate*, and I seem to recall it was warm outside but not enough to explain my soaked-through clothing by the time I arrived in SoHo. Clearly I was circling the drain, and my friend was a gracious hostess—she'd gotten some takeout and gave me a nice glass of wine—but I rarely heard from her again once I'd dished my side of the whole lurid saga. Ditto a couple of other writer acquaintances who bombarded me with emails during the first days of my scandal and enticed me to meet them and talk about things; details of one such conversation appeared in a scurrilous article written by a third party who taught at the same college with one of these acquaintances. As for the various other writers, editors, reporters, professors, and publishing people I'd known—well, for the most part they simply vanished into the ether, nor did I find myself missing their ethereal companionship.

But Christopher and William weren't the only nice exceptions among literary/media folk. The "worldly woman in publishing," to whom I'd once confided about Mya and certain others, remains a friend. Nowadays she's a literary agent, let's call her Leslie, and during our first post-scandal dinner I asked her to be my agent, at least for a while—*not* because I expected to go on as a viable author, at least not anytime soon, but rather because I needed a proper agent to deal with my now-very-skittish European publishers for *Philip Roth*. Leslie promised to run it by the people at her agency; if nothing else, she thought maybe she could do odd jobs for me on the low. Um, no. Her proposal vis-à-vis colleagues was met with a collective *gasp*—just that—as though she'd wondered aloud whether it would be OK if she reversed the earth's orbit.

And that was the main message: I Was Canceled. Done. Stick a fork in me. "Blake," said Paul, the last of my writer friends who remained loyal, "the life you knew is *over*. Forever. The sooner you accept that, the better."

"Fuck them all," said my mother, who lived with her cats in the sticks outside Norman, Oklahoma, and didn't follow newspapers or the internet; I'd had to explain things to her, exhaustively. "Just fuck 'em, sweetie, and come home. I'm gonna die soon, and you can have my house and whatever's left of my money."

Good old Marlies, and thank whatever gods there be that my saintly old pal, Dr. Matt, spared me the hellishness of actually having to live with her and vice versa. (In a moment of Lady Bountiful ebullience, Sandra had once imagined the possibility—"We love Marlies!"—of having my mother live in their nicely appointed bunkhouse at Breeze Hill. "That would last about fifteen minutes," said Burck, "before the squad cars began to arrive.") Matt texted me photos of his pool and tennis court—"the view"—and said his garage apartment was all mine if I wanted it. I hit the road for Oklahoma the very next day.

Burck hoped to cheer us both up with a long father-and-son weekend at the swanky Adolphus Hotel in Dallas ("where I've stayed many a time in my pursuit of justice"), coinciding with my fifty-eighth birthday that summer. Sandra's speech was mostly incomprehensible now, and she communicated by writing things on a pad that sometimes didn't make much sense either. My father had finally persuaded her to let him hire a helper, and thus he'd hopefully planned our little trip, but it fell through a couple of weeks before my birthday: "Sandra has become increasingly despondent of late," Burck emailed me on June 13. "This morning she wrote: 'I am slipping into depression. I feel like killing myself.'" Burck had called the Suicide Hotline and spoken with a counselor via speaker phone so Sandra could listen; the crisis was averted, but he'd locked up his gun closet and hidden the key, and was now resigned to staying home for the most part and keeping an eye on her, helper or no. "I'm having a hard time," he wanly noted in closing, while bearing in mind that his son was another suicide risk: "I am so sorry about your travails. Try to stay hopeful and drive with great care."

He knew I was even then returning from a nightmare trip to my former home in Virginia. (I'd read his email while stopping for gas in Vinita, of all places, just before the last leg of my journey back to Oklahoma City.) The main reason for the trip was melancholy enough—I had to gather up and organize, under duress, the vast papers Roth had left in my care over the years. On June 4, the *New York Times* had published a piece ("What Happens to Philip Roth's Legacy Now?") about the potentially irrevocable damage my scandal had done to Roth's literary (and otherwise) reputation, and some little anxiety had been aired about wresting his papers away from the miscreant (me) so that a proper biography could be undertaken by an author of proven morals. Thus the Roth Estate insisted I return the papers immediately, despite Roth's own provision that I be given "eighteen months after publication" to do the job right. I was too demoralized not to oblige.

While I was in my empty old house (FOR SALE), alone, a scabrous article dropped in the *Virginian Pilot* about my alleged philandering/"abuse" among students and colleagues during my years at ODU. Two or three weeks before, my lawyer had gone over the *Pilot*'s list of allegations with me and filtered my reply to the effect that they were categorically vicious, deranged bullshit, a conclusion that ODU's lawyers had reached after their own investigation. At first we thought the lawyers would persuade the *Pilot* to kill the story, but it was hot copy and the *Pilot* decided to run it anyway with the proviso that the lawyers' own report—refuting the allegations as "flatly false" or at best unsubstantiated—would also be printed in full. So the story broke while I was in town packing up Roth's papers, and that night I had to explain to my daughter—with whom I was dining at a downtown restaurant, a bad idea but I had to get out of that haunted house of ours—why the mother of a Burton School student in our old carpool was giving me such a conspicuous stink-eye from yonder booth. I was trying to be cheerful and amusing for my daughter's sake, a gruesome ordeal (never mind what it was like for her), and meanwhile my rage was the only thing keeping me from cutting my throat. When I insisted to my lawyer that, by God, *this* time I meant to sue the bastards, he sensibly assured me that the *Pilot* would like nothing better than to go toe to toe with a #MeToo pariah. Meanwhile, too, this latest wrinkle had been picked up by the national and international press—"SEX PEST" read the *Daily Mail* headline—and the impending foreign editions of *Philip Roth* were now at risk of cancelation too, and I wasn't sure how I'd go on eating without the money they owed me on publication.

BURCK KNEW THAT his eighty-seventh birthday on August 22 might well be his last, and also that we needed to reconcile as a family, if possible, since better late than never. I was daunted by the prospect of facing my stepfamily after seventeen years—all the more given my squalid notoriety—but heartened by my daughter's company when the time came. Our airport shuttle from Albuquerque arrived late at La Fonda hotel near the Santa Fe Plaza, where we were met by a sweet-natured friend/factotum of Burck and Sandra, Pablo, who drove us the five minutes or so to their posh neighborhood, Las Barrancas. Burck had directed us to let ourselves into his house—a house I knew only from a video tour he'd emailed me after his first visit to Virginia in 2014—where he and Sandra would be sleeping at that hour;

following his instructions, we found the guest wing, lighted on our right, with its two separate bedrooms and bathroom in between.

The next morning I tapped on my daughter's door and found her awake and looking at her phone. We gave each other comically anxious bug-eyed looks.

"Here we go," I said, blowing out my cheeks. "Ready to meet Sandra? I'll go first and kinda break the ice, but don't leave me hangin' . . ."

My daughter assured me she wouldn't, and I ventured into the kitchen where Burck and Sandra were waiting. Sandra clapped rapidly to show she was pleased, and I gave her a hug; she was frailer even than my father, proverbial skin and bones, whereas Burck looked wizened but jaunty in a tweed vest he liked to wear most days. Amid the burble of greeting Sandra tried to say something—a pleasantry, no doubt, that came out sounding like the protest of a wounded animal. Burck's face went solemn as he tried to parse whatever she wanted to say, but, thank God, my daughter chose that moment to present herself and was happily received by all.

MY STEPSIBLINGS WOULDN'T arrive until later that afternoon, and meanwhile Burck drove the four of us around Santa Fe, where we visited the Museum of Indian Arts and Culture and had lunch at a popular outdoor burger joint. At the latter—small world—I bumped into the wealthy, vivacious old pal who'd been keeping me afloat in Oklahoma City with ghostwriting assignments for his philanthropic foundation and other interests. He was in Santa Fe for the opera, and he and Burck discussed that beloved cultural institution and a few common acquaintances back home. Sandra sat at a separate picnic table and glared at her phone.

My daughter was tired after a long day of being upbeat and charming—and facing more of the same once my step-siblings arrived—so she went to lie down that afternoon. I think Sandra did likewise, or maybe she did what she usually did when left to her devices: putter around the kitchen while a news channel murmured on the little TV. Anyway Burck and I retired to a corner of his lovely, spacious patio—gardens, urns, elaborate tile work—and had our first actual chat, just the two of us, in a long time. He hadn't been able to travel because of Sandra's frailty, and, while we emailed almost daily, we rarely spoke on the phone anymore because of his deafness—"consequence of firing thousands of rounds from a 30 caliber M-1 without any ear protection in my long ago Army days," he wrote me. He could get by with the help of high-powered hearing aids, all the better if there was no ambient noise and his interlocutor had a deep voice and could look at him while speaking.

Burck seemed at peace with the world that day. He too was tired after exerting himself as a host and now sat almost recumbent in his lounge chair, mostly just listening while I filled him in on my latest setbacks. While walking around museums and chatting that morning, his face had become drawn and his wheezing more pronounced; but now, relaxing at last, he struck me as almost boyish—hardly a line on his face and jaunty, I repeat, in his well-worn vest.

I aired something of my dread at the prospect of meeting

Kelli and Aaron after all these years. What must they think of me now, I wondered, given that their opinion had been low enough seventeen years ago, prior to being corroborated by the wider world? Or maybe they were unaware of the worst . . . ? Burck felt obliged to disabuse me on that point.

"I can assure you they're quite aware of things," he said, and put a hand on my arm: "It'll be fine. They take their cues from their mother."

By this I assume he meant the woman who'd welcomed me with friendly clapping, and not so much the enigmatic person who poignantly avoided social interaction by staring at her phone, or who walked twenty yards behind us, with the dog, during our morning stroll with her and Burck. My heart went out to her, and I wanted almost as badly as Burck for us to be reconciled here at the end. Anyway it was a lovely summer day in the mountains, and we were having a nice chat just the two of us, and that would have to suffice for now and perhaps forever.

My father was smiling when he said, "Sandra had a lot of good friends here, but she doesn't want to see them anymore, and I can't leave her alone. So our world has become very small."

KELLI AND AARON and Aaron's partner, Kelly with a y, arrived around five, and we gathered on the patio with their next-door neighbor Julie. I would have liked a martini, but nobody drank liquor in that crowd—not even Burck, whose bum pancreas had finally compelled him to phase out spirits. So we sipped wine and chatted. I took a deep breath and approached my stepsister for the first time in seventeen years.

"You look exactly the same as the last time I saw you," I said, sincerely enough.

"So do you," she said, which wasn't true but I let it pass with a *pshaw* or some such. She smiled receptively.

What did we talk about? I asked questions about her daughters, and what she herself was doing (interior design). I didn't expect reciprocal curiosity—especially given the squalor of my life—and I didn't get it. I sensed I was in the midst of a kind of kabuki for my father's benefit. Sandra clapped happily in his presence, or (at worst) drifted behind with the dog so that (perhaps?) he could chat with me and my daughter unencumbered; but when I found myself alone with her, it was sticky as ever. Just before her children arrived that evening, she'd emerged from her bedroom wearing a simple but elegant outfit—she and her kids had always been snappy dressers—and I took a stab at courtly admiration:

"You look wonderful, Sandra!"

She nodded austerely, waited for me to say more, then walked on when I could think of nothing more to say.

But everybody was nice to my daughter, and that was enough for me. Burck had often heard her sing during his trips to Virginia—she was training as a mezzo-soprano at an arts magnet school—and he'd begged her to sing an aria before his birthday dinner that night. After the pre-prandial mingling, then, she cued up the accompaniment to "Voi che sapete" on her laptop. I'm always charmed by how the demands of performance transform my shy daughter; standing in Burck's big raftered living room, waiting for her first note, she abruptly became Cherubino with an impish wink and smirk. Sandra and her children listened with bright kabuki smiles, Julie the neighbor gave me a nodding *Heyyy! She's good* look, whereas Burck was simply radiant with delight. Seeing him thus made me almost wish I'd been his granddaughter instead of his leftover son from a disastrous first family—but, qua the latter at least, I had a connection with him that nobody else on earth could ever have.

Nine of our old high school chums communicate via a group text thread, and I think all of us would agree it's nice but pretty banal: sports/political commentary, birthday wishes, nostalgia. When my scandal blew up, the only other writer in our group (the one who accurately informed me that my old life was *over*) started a separate thread that excluded me so they could frankly discuss things among themselves. The only exchange on this alt thread that I was privy to, thanks to Matt, occurred just after the ODU story broke in the *Pilot*, when one of our friends wondered whether they were doing me any favors by pretending, as ever, that I was just one of the boys (plus one girl: Jennifer), given that I seemed to have some pretty ugly issues or else why would this stuff keep coming up—? For his part Matt had seen at close range how hard I was taking things—not only that shit-on-my-grave *Pilot* piece and all that went with it, but also my divorce, my daughter's distress, my mother's worsening senility, my father's failing health, my financial woes, add your own topping(s)—and sternly advised our friends via the alt thread (whereof he shared only that part with me over a drink) that they should review the ODU lawyers' published rebuttal of those gleeful *Pilot* slanders, and moreover Matt assured them that I'd accepted a seemly degree of culpability and was trying to get on with some kind of life withal, and the last thing on earth I needed was my oldest friends adding their weight to the pile-on. Whereupon (so far as I know) the alt thread went silent for good.

One of my high school girlfriends, Alice, is on a similar text thread with her own chums from the Class of '82, one year below us. When Alice and I met for dinner, shortly after I returned to Oklahoma, she told me how she and her friends had texted one another about seeing me on *Morning Joe* (or whatever) when *Philip Roth* was published, how everybody was so excited and happy for me, etc.—then *boom* . . . and a long wondering bemusement ensued. I see this bemusement in the faces of old acquaintances on the rare-enough occasion I go to some larger gathering like a wedding. Everybody Knows—that's a given—but of course they fix smiles on their faces and try to act as if they haven't seen a ghost. Which is what I am essentially: a ghost, leading a posthumous life. Oh, it's not all bad. Relieved of strenuous old ambitions, I try to savor the simple pleasures of being alive in the biological sense: I have my little sanity rituals, I sleep more, I swim and whack tennis balls (thanks to Matt), I cook and eat nice meals. I see old friends like Alice—one of the nice people in my life who no longer has that what-do-you-say-to-a-rapist look.

MY LAST ZOOM interview—almost a daily chore back in the days surrounding my book release—was with a nice Italian litterateur, Francesco Chiamulera, a month or so after my scandal broke. Oh, and I should add here that all European editions of *Philip Roth* were duly published, and the media over there—especially in Italy and Spain for whatever reason—were wonderfully humane compared to the nonstop ass-stomping I got in the States. They didn't badger me to "admit what [I] did" when I put aside the sackcloth and ashes for a moment and tried to defend myself against some of the more grotesque allegations. In Europe, along with mostly glowing reviews of *Philip Roth*, there were a few editorials pointing out that I'd never been formally charged with any crime and, besides, what did any of it have to do with the merits of my book? Likewise, during our hour-long Zoom chat, Francesco spent the first fifty-two minutes asking me intelligent, decorous questions about Roth and my biography, until he politely inquired how I'd first found out that W. W. Norton was scuttling publication (Answer: via the *New York Times*, like everybody else) and what did I think of all that? Whereupon I naturally said I was appalled and pointed out that Norton was holding me to the standard of Caesar's wife, and every writer in the world should be unnerved by the implications—etc.

At the time I'd only just moved into Matt's garage apartment and hadn't gotten my own Wi-Fi, so I had to do the interview in Matt's study, where the router was located. Matt's a serious art collector, and over my left shoulder (as I only discovered when Francesco sent me a low-res video the next day) is a lovely but rather erotic Art Nouveau statuette of a female nude. So people will say I'm up to my old tricks. And here's another thing: when I rushed over to the main house to do the interview, I interrupted Matt's sixteen-year-old son in the act of fixing his breakfast. I've known all three of Matt's kids since birth and used to have lively friendships with them, ditto with the delightful offspring of my other old friends—the sort of thing my Lusher colleague Steve Burt meant, I think, when he remembered (in *Slate*) that I used to "entertain [my students] with witty banter": "It wasn't unwholesome. It was kind of nice to see." But of course wholesomeness is in the eye of the beholder. In her email reply to Barbara Jakobson, my Twitter slagger invoked yet another friend of a friend who'd allegedly known me in my Lusher days and hence witnessed my grooming of students "in real time"—which I'm pretty sure was the same behavior Steve was trying to describe in more charitable terms. Another nice Italian, Antonio Monda, asked me about the "grooming" allegations for his *La Repubblica* interview, and what follows is roughly half of my original answer in English, which my lawyer gutted to four words for publication ("I categorically deny them"):

> Prior to this ordeal, "grooming" was a word I associated with personal hygiene. I stayed in touch with some of my former students, male and female, because they stayed in touch with me; while they were in high school, I left the balls in their courts if they wanted to catch up over coffee or whatever. Later, when they were legal adults, I had sex with a few of them. That was almost twenty years ago. Now that I'm the father of a (mortified and grief-stricken) daughter, I find my behavior disgusting to put it mildly. But I did nothing illegal. And it bears mentioning—as my former principal also pointed out—that there were no complaints against me during my seven-year career as a

middle-school teacher, and in 2000 I was honored at the governor's mansion as Humanities Teacher of the Year. So I must have done something right.

This is a roundabout way of saying that I no longer have affectionate bantering attachments with young people other than my daughter, and when I encountered Matt's son that day in the kitchen en route to my interview with Francesco, we were polite but a little constrained with each other. I repeat: Everybody Knows, and what do you do with that information . . . ?

Chapter Fifteen

FLUTTERING
IN THE WIND

The gods permitted my father that last happy birthday in Santa Fe, then swiftly moved in for the kill. A couple of weeks after our departure, he reported that Sandra had fainted on the back patio; since he didn't have the strength to lift her—though it would have been like lifting a large water fowl at that point—he summoned an ambulance to take her to the ER, where she eventually came to after various meds and infusions. On top of the dementia, aphasia, and occasional suicidal depression, she was found to be suffering from painful sinus infections and worsening hypertension. Meanwhile her usual doctor couldn't see her for at least two months, such was the crazy demand in a smallish city with so many affluent retirees. "Long day's journey into night," Burck's email concluded.

But his own deterioration was even more precipitous. "This old guy has been dealing with a nagging cough for a couple of months that has gotten progressively worse," he wrote me on September 25, 2021. A chest X-ray had found "suspected pleural effusion," and he was sent to get a contrast-enhanced CT scan to see whether he had actual pneumonia, which turned out to be too hopeful. In addition to the "large necrotic mass in the left lower lobe most worrisome for primary lung cancer," the radiologist also noted—why not?—the presence of "severe thoracic degenerative disc disease": "I coulda told him *that*," Burck quipped.

Apprised of my father's almost certain death sentence, I tried to get hold of his primary care physician, only to learn that nobody but Sandra was on his HIPAA list and hence privy to his medical information. So I permitted myself a rare phone call to Burck, who seemed in decent spirits despite the fact that he was very evidently dying. In the movies, characters who are dying tend to speak in halting voices, as though choosing their last words with exquisite care. Ever since listening to my dying father speak, I'm aware of how rare it is for an actor to get this right. It's not enough to add those faltering little pauses; you have to talk as though every word is like a heavy waterlogged sack you're dragging behind you. Speaking becomes hard work, like everything else.

"If everybody would just leave me alone on a desert island," Burck said in that vinyl-record-at-half-speed voice, "I'd be *fine*. It's having to be *on* for people that takes it out of me."

The main person he had to be *on* for was his stepdaughter—the person he could least bear to hurt, so there was no question of telling her to go away and leave him alone already. Besides, somebody had to drive him to those inconclusive biopsies, and by default that was either Kelli or Julie the neighbor. And while the results were pending, Kelli assured me that Burck looked even worse than he sounded, which is when I began waking most mornings with my heart pounding out of my chest while I wondered whether he was alive another day, and what a burden every step and syllable must be for him now. Later I saw the rumpled blanket on the sofa in his Santa Fe study, his cane propped at the end, and imagined him retiring there earlier and earlier each day, after knocking out a few more lines of his obit and replying to my latest worried email.

It was having to *imagine* his suffering that I couldn't quite bear at that point in my ruined life; it would be better, I figured, if I could be there and experience the reality firsthand, until it became more mundane. After my father's second biopsy, then, I decided to put my foot down—diffidently, I thought. Deploring "this gauntlet of biopsies," I offered to phone the oncologist myself and force his hand to get on with some kind of effective treatment. Also I proposed a three-day visit: I would stay at an Airbnb, I wrote, and "come to Monte Alto [his street in Las Barrancas] when you say, and help out with whatever needs doing, and above all have a chance to talk with you alone. Again, if you vehemently object to a visit I have to respect your wishes, but such a response would frankly hurt my feelings at this point." That whiney last line makes me wince now, but I'd proposed other visits and he'd repeatedly asked me to leave him alone (despite my stepsister's frequent presence) until he felt better, as though he were recovering from lung cancer rather than dying from it.

His reply came within the hour:

> I vehemently object. Please do not call Drs. —— or
> ——. Stay out of it. I've not been given treatment
> because they don't yet know what the treatment
> should be.
>
> Also, please respond to my invitation to visit, not
> yours. I want to be feeling right for a visit. I'll know
> when that is. It's not now. Please respect my wishes.
>
> Also, put a pause on the emails.

ONE OF THE THINGS I had in common with Philip Roth (aside from lechery) was an obsessiveness toward the task at hand, whatever it may be. This made me a good literary biographer, I like to think, and a sometimes insufferable human being. Whenever my agent or editor hadn't returned an important (?) phone call or email within a few hours, or I hadn't been paid right away by this or that vendor, or felt I was being slighted (however subtly) by a friend, I would present the case to my lucid wife, who would nicely contextualize things and persuade me to chill the fuck out. At the distance of two years now, and with a somewhat more tranquil frame of mind, I can read Burck's "vehemently object" email and grasp his wish to be left in peace—this while I sigh at the gaucherie of my having badgered him in the first place. But at the time I lapsed into a panic of self-loathing—even helpless, dying, my father could reduce me to that—and all I could think to do was run the whole business by my estranged wife, who now lived half a continent away and didn't speak to me if she could help it.

Her reply was frank but charitable, as expected. That I was butting into a situation I understood imperfectly (at best) went without saying, but she permitted herself to say it, and also to remind me that it was hardly the first time I'd become indignant/fretful in the face of uncertainty and forced other people, who have their own problems, to explain things and placate me. Which wears a body down. My hurt feelings were not Burck's foremost concern at the moment, she continued, nor should they be; also I'd caused him (and he was far from alone in this) a lot of pain and worry and shame these last few months, and he likely didn't want to be reminded of all that. He'd already made it clear that he loved me, and I should be thankful for that final birthday visit and his sympathy in general. And now, well, he may or may not wish to see me again before he died, but in any case I should hold on to the good things and bear in mind that life is rarely perfect.

So I gave Burck space for as long as I could reasonably stand it—three days—all the while knowing his grip on life was loosening like that of poor, grimacing Cary Grant, in *North by Northwest*, clinging to the side of Mount Rushmore while Martin Landau gleefully stamps on his fingers. And I knew too—I felt it in my morning panics—that our latest contretemps was a burr in his heart as it was in mine, but his cussedness would keep him grimly silent if I didn't break the ice one more time. I hesitated to acknowledge that his life was all but over—even while he persevered with those fucking biopsies—but I couldn't avoid the implication entirely. "Papa," I wrote him on November 10:

> This is just to say that it's very hard to know someone you love is suffering, and not be able to do anything about it. Also this: your re-entering my life seven and a half years ago—and getting to know and love [my daughter] and vice versa—meant the world to me, and it would break my heart for us to end in estrangement.
>
> Let me leave it at this: if you need anything, I'm here for you. And I hope the oxygen and antibiotics are helping you feel better.

Not only was Burck prompt in his reply, but it was the longest email he'd written me in months. The plans he set forth scarcely acknowledged the recent strife between us or any possibility of his dying in the foreseeable future:

> I thought it would be a good idea to discuss upcoming holidays. I assume you would like to spend either Thanksgiving or Christmas with your mother—and she would expect the latter.
>
> I am programmed to know the results of my camera biopsy on November 19. I should (hopefully) be able to discuss treatment options thereafter. Your evaluation will be carefully weighed by me. So, you may want to come to SF on Monday, Nov. 22. . . .
>
> We can have all the time alone you want. I have an appointment with Dr. ——— at 10 am on Tuesday,

Nov. 23rd, but no appointments thereafter. You are
welcome to stay through Thanksgiving weekend if
you choose. You should know that sometimes I'm
more focused than others; but I think you already
know that. . . . Love, Papa

The "camera" biopsy was his third, and, according to Kelli,
by far the most painful: they popped a vein trying to insert
an IV, and afterward Burck began to die in earnest. On the
last day of his life, Kelli would check online and see that
the results of his previous, *second* biopsy were still pending. I may be wrong, but knowing how certain doctors had
gaslighted Cheever, say, through his own cancer travails, I
get the impression Burck's oncologist was basically running
out the clock.

I accepted Burck's Thanksgiving invitation with almost weeping gratitude, and promptly reserved an Airbnb for the dates he'd mentioned so I wouldn't be too much underfoot on Monte Alto. But then came my stepbrother's early-morning text four days later—the first text he'd sent me in seventeen years, so it wasn't hard to anticipate the gist—whereupon I threw some things in a bag and hit the road for Santa Fe. I remember little of the drive. I'd left before breakfast and found myself ravenous by noon, so I stopped at a barbecue takeout place in the Texas panhandle. I waited five or ten minutes for my food, then blurted out to the doe-eyed girl taking orders, "My father's dying in Santa Fe! I have to hurry!"

It was dark by the time I arrived, and Kelli was waiting for me on a bench in the foyer. Aaron and Kelly with a y wouldn't arrive until the next day. Seeing the stricken look on my stepsister's face, I worried I was too late, but she was just reeling from the all-day ordeal of arranging hospice care, comforting her mother, and tending a beloved, dying stepfather. For the first time in decades, and perhaps the last time ever, she seemed happy to see me. We hugged, sniffling, and she led me back to the room where I'd stayed for Burck's eighty-seventh birthday—the same room where he used to watch late-night Westerns and tipple bourbon until fairly recently, and now the room in which he'd seen fit to die. The family portrait taken shortly after his marriage to Sandra in 1981—the only one with me (but not Scott) in it—hung on a wall there, as I imagine Sandra wouldn't have wanted a reminder of my existence in their actual master bedroom.

Burck had stayed somewhat conscious, and kept his hearing aids in, until I arrived, and the first thing we did was take him to the toilet. Kelli and I stood on either side of that rumpled paper bag of a body and basically carried him along, then she left us to it and I closed the door behind her. At first I put Burck on the toilet, but he preferred to stand, like a man, so I held him upright by the armpits.

"Fuck. Goddammit," he said, when he missed the bowl and piddled on our feet. What he hated worst was the indignity of it all, and I worried he was cursing *me* for not holding him closer to the bowl or whatever. Anyway we got it done, and I helped him back to bed.

I ventured a smile, looking down at him, and said, "You don't look so bad, Papa."

His eyes were wide and staring, as though he were trying to see me better or perhaps see something behind me. "Blake," he said at last. "I'm just fluttering in the wind."

In the foyer Kelli had mentioned that her teenage daughters were coming from California and New York respectively—the older, Beau, was a sophomore at NYU—and I asked Burck whether he wanted us to bring them to his bedside when they arrived.

"Absolutely *not*," he groaned, shaking his head slowly but vehemently.

He'd come to love these two girls once they'd emerged

from the worst of their feral brattiness, and for that reason, I imagine, he didn't want to endure the hard, hard work involved in showing the full measure of his devotion. Also— as my daughter summed it up when I felt obliged to ask *her* whether she wanted to get on a plane to Santa Fe—"Burck wouldn't want me to remember him that way." Instead she sat right down and wrote an email that I read aloud to him, stentorian, so he could hear. Without alluding to the occasion for her note, she told him what "a wonderful and kind presence in [her] life" he'd always been and assured him of her undying love in about a hundred perfect words.

"That's wonderful," said Burck. "She's *wonderful*."

I can't recall whether he was still awake when Beau and Belle arrived and made a beeline for his bedside—understandably, given the distance they'd traveled. In any case, he heroically roused himself and somehow managed to raise his arms to embrace them and croon "Beauty girl! Beauty girl!"—one for each girl. I thought maybe these would be his last words, the equivalent of the shorn, dying Samson collapsing the temple with a last triumphal push.

BUT THE NEXT MORNING, my God, he not only woke up but *sat* up and asked for coffee. I held off canceling my Airbnb for Thanksgiving; maybe he'd live a while longer; hell, maybe we'd all gather again, even more felicitously, for his eighty-eighth birthday. The only sign he was still dying was the way he kept his eyes closed while sipping coffee and saying this and that, smiling the while, the better to reassure us that he was indeed on the uptick. Again I worried the rigors of conviviality would be the literal death of him, and offered to read him the newspaper. Sandra looked at me and nodded encouragingly, and the others followed her out of the room.

After I'd read something about the UN Climate Summit, Burck sipped his coffee and wisely commented (eyes closed à la the blind prophet Tiresias): "Blake, the damage is already *done*, and even if it weren't, do you really think countries like China— . . ."

On he went (slowly), and I agreed with pretty much every word of it and said so. Next I read something about internecine squabbling among Democrats, and again he lucidly remarked on the party's self-defeating idiocies (especially among so-called progressives) such as Defund the Police, etc. Here at the end, at least ideologically, we were in all but perfect accord.

After half an hour or so he began falling asleep again, when a hospice nurse arrived to give him a sponge bath. She was a pretty Hispanic woman with very little English, and she went about her task with a solemn, tender deliberation that made Burck groan with pleasure. Slowly, carefully, she ran the big warm sponge along both his arms, washed his hair, and gave him a shave. That a dying man could be made to feel so good was heartening to see.

"He still responds to a woman's touch," said Kelli, who knew and understood that aspect of my father. Not for the first time I was struck by her worldliness on the one hand and a kind of intransigent cluelessness on the other, as when the hospice counselor called us together in the kitchen to discuss how things should go down. She explained how much morphine we should give him—more and more, of course, as the hours dragged on—and at some point wondered whether Burck would want some kind of spiritual solace.

The answer was No or even Fuck No, but Kelli was galvanized and began holding forth about the various ways we could help ease his spirit into the Great Beyond. Sandra rolled her eyes at me and shook her head, and I was reminded that we weren't so far apart in certain ways and might have been friends in some better world.

I NEEDED A BREAK after that and walked the mile or so down a steep hill to a road near the Plaza where (I was told) there was a good place for brunch with a pleasant patio. I ordered an enormous plate of Eggs Royale and sat reading the booklet the hospice counselor had left. Dying, I learned, was a process that begins long before the dying person is even aware of it, like a slow leak, and tends to entail an almost unconscious retreat from the world, a paring away of extraneous things. Burck, I reflected, had been dying for quite a while now.

When I returned, Kelli buttonholed me in a blandly officious way that meant she was dissembling hostility or at least distaste. Now that Beau and Belle were here, she said, they would need the spare room where I'd slept the night before.

"Really, I can sleep just about anywhere," I said, rather than point out that Kelli had her own pied-à-terre in town and could easily put them up there.

"I was thinking an Airbnb."

I immediately agreed and broke out my laptop to make arrangements. For a moment I'd wondered whether she meant to dismiss me altogether, in which case we might have had that open, raucous squabble we arguably should have had years ago to clear some of the fetid air between us. But an Airbnb? Sure, no problem. I was going broke at the time and could have easily crashed on a couch without bothering anybody, but I could see that a room of one's own was worth draining a few more coins out of the old coffer.

SO KELLI'S FRIENDLINESS didn't quite last, but her mother seemed to be trying, at least, to let bygones be bygones. At one point I was reading on a sofa in the living room, when I felt a pinch on my stockinged toe and there was Sandra, waggling my foot and giving me a charming little conspiratorial smile, which I returned with interest. Later I left to check-in at my Airbnb—a perfectly adequate room with kitchenette in a working-class Hispanic neighborhood on the other side of town—then returned to my father's bedside after dark. Kelli and her daughters had filled the room with candles, to appease the spirits perhaps, and at some point Sandra wandered in, looked around, then sat on the other side of the bed and stared at me. I was weeping a little and wondered whether she was trying to determine the actual extent of my grief. For a moment I stared back at her and smiled, sadly but a little sternly too, as if to say "I have a right to be here, and you're welcome to stay and stare at me, but I'm not going anywhere. You've had him to yourself long enough." But I don't think she contested my presence; maybe she was wondering who her husband's only surviving son really *was* . . . or maybe—probably—she was just in her own world and beyond worrying about the relative impoliteness of staring at people.

I think it was the next day that Burck went to the toilet for the last time—or rather to a little commode (provided by the hospice people) right there in his room. I was reading on the patio when Kelly with a y appeared at the sliding door and said that Burck needed to relieve himself and wanted me to help him. My stepbrother was around, so I was touched that Burck had assigned this intimate chore to me.

He was mostly beyond talking, though he still groaned a little (with pleasure, during his second sponge bath that morning) or grunted when we moved him for whatever reason, and his hearing aids were out and would stay out, so there was no point in conversing. Also there was no question of holding him upright while he peed, since he was too unsteady and the stream would have splashed all over the place. So I lowered him gently onto the commode, and he sat there, collapsed, a withered gourd. Things were not ending well for either of us, I thought; on the other hand, we'd both enjoyed a measure of success in life that we hadn't really expected, and here we were together at the end— after so much sorrow and misunderstanding. It could have been worse.

Anyway that was it for the commode. Burck was too weak and fragile to move, and a male hospice nurse offered to catheterize him. Remind me not to get catheterized while

I'm dying. Like a plumber toiling over a tricky widget, the nurse tried and tried to jab a biggish rubber tube into Burck's urethra, while the dying man grimaced and groaned and curled his hands. Shakily I asked the nurse to use more lubricant, but Kelli put her foot down.

"We don't need this. Just stop. Stop. He can get by with a diaper. It's not like he's drinking a lot of water at this point."

And of course she was right. Again I marveled at her clear-eyed competence when it came to Burck's bodily well-being, and certain practical matters otherwise, but again, too, I was reminded of her woo-woo inanity when, a bit later, she rousted me out of Burck's room, where I sat in the corner quietly working on my laptop and keeping an eye on him.

We were all convened in the living room, where Kelli stood shivering and rubbing her arms as if to wipe ecto-plasm off her fingers. "OK, you guys—whew—I'm getting some *very* strong signals in there . . ."

From the spirits, she meant, who were gathering in force now that Burck was about to depart. She pointed contemp-tuously at my laptop: "No more media in the room. And we need to take our shoes off . . ."

There was more, but I forget. When she was done, I repaired to the kitchen table with my laptop. Kelli's younger daughter, Belle, approached me and shyly offered a piece of gingerbread from a nice bakery in town.

AS FOR MY STEPBROTHER, he was pleasant enough and saw to it that we had enormous meals for dinner each night of

Burck's dying. He was a tall, muscular fellow who'd inherited his mother's delicate facial features and his father's temperament—think Bill Clinton: jovial-seeming but laser-focused on his own interests—whereas his sister looked more like her father but was Sandra's daughter down to her toenails.

"So how's it going?" he asked me one night, while the dinner was heating and I sat in the living room poring over my father's impressive "CV" file.

It was the first and only hint of curiosity either he or Kelli had deigned to show me since reappearing in my life, and I began to answer with a serious account of things: "Well, it's been quite an ordeal. I went from the happiest I've ever been to losing just about everything within a few hours . . ."—then I saw he was only passing time until dinner was ready. So I cut my spiel short with the usual remark I make at such moments: ". . . but my daughter still loves me, so it could be worse."

He spoke of his own rather serious legal troubles some years ago and how he'd managed to bounce back, and indeed I found a dram of comfort in his hard-won sangfroid. When I asked about his former wife—the one I'd known and liked seventeen years ago—he chuckled and said, "If she saw me now on the sidewalk, she'd run me over."

And we laughed. My own kindly, judicious ex-wife would refrain from that sort of thing, though (in certain moods) she'd have to think about it first.

THAT AFTERNOON, SHORTLY after Kelli's spirit meeting, we'd gathered around Burck's bed (our shoes removed) and waited for him to die. The oxygen machine hissed and gurgled out in the hall, and Burck's breaths were ragged snarls further and further apart. We sat there thinking our private Burck thoughts, sniffling, alert to the longer intervals of silence when he seemed to have breathed his last . . . but no. Finally we agreed he had a few more hours of life in him and dispersed around the house or back to an Airbnb (me) to regroup.

After the usual enormous dinner, Kelli and Aaron proposed that we commemorate Burck's passing by writing our various regrets—about life in general, that is—on little pieces of paper and burning them in the fire.

"That's a whole flaming book or two for me," I said, or some such; nobody laughed because it wasn't funny and adverted to the squalor of my life. Anyway the others wrote down their regrets and burned them in the fire, one by one, until I felt a boredom so noxious I worried I might actually lose my mind and longed to be anywhere on earth but where I was at that moment. With what I hoped was a look of weary, good-humored benignity, I said I was calling it a night and stood to go, whereupon Kelli informed me that she and Belle (Beau was already on a plane back to New York) would be staying at her pied-à-terre that night, whereas Aaron and Kelly were going back to Bishop's Lodge, so that left me on deathwatch. Which was fine—wonderful really—since I much preferred to be alone with my father when he died.

I retired to the room opposite Burck's and started to watch a movie on my laptop. Around nine o'clock I heard the others leave, and a few minutes later I heard the desultory slap-slap of Sandra's slippers as she wandered off to bed. Just to be sure, I stayed put for another few minutes before checking on Burck. His room was dark. The oxygen machine gurgled and chugged but there was no snarling accompaniment from my father. With a shaky hand I groped for the switch on his bedside lamp, bracing myself for the sight of Burck's corpse, but the lamp wouldn't turn on. Kelli and her kids must have unplugged it because of the candles. I got down on my hands and knees, searching for the cord with the help of my phone flashlight, and finally plugged it in.

"The dead look so terribly dead when they're dead," says Larry Darrell in *The Razor's Edge*. Truer words, boy. Burck hardly looked like Burck anymore: he looked like a simulacrum, a generic cadaver. His face, his body, had subtly deflated and left a wan, waxen shell. No wonder Jessica Mitford had so gleefully mocked the American ritual of spiffing up corpses with rouges and powders until they look like whorish dolls. I felt a fresh respect for Burck's refusal to subject himself to the final indignity of a funeral. I tried to close his mouth—it looked a bit more like Burck that way—but the jaw kept falling open, and I gave up.

"Burck's dead," I began to text my stepsiblings, then (remembering Kelli) I emended this to "Burck has passed."

"OH BURCK, I should have been here!" Kelli shrieked, and flung herself on the bed like a Hindu widow diving into her husband's funeral pyre. Burck himself would have rolled his eyes at this—even vis-à-vis Kelli—and I permitted myself a rare expression of pique, something like:

"Oh c'mon, Kelli. You did everything you could, but now he's dead. Enough."

She remained face down on the bed, but I assume she heard this and filed it away for later contemplation. Aaron, Kelly, and Belle stood respectfully in the background. I was lying next to Burck, or rather Burck's body, my right hand just touching his left arm through the blanket. I felt no sense of an abiding presence, and yet I felt a protective/comforting something-or-other, what a child feels clutching a teddy bear.

Aaron and Kelli woke their mother and brought her in to say goodbye. I got off the bed and stood in the opposite corner. Mutely Sandra palpated the body under the sheets, rather like an ape finding its dead mate and trying to puzzle out why it won't move or answer—and I mean no irreverence by this. I found it far more poignant than Kelli's carrying on. When Sandra was certain her mate was no more, she got into bed beside him and lay staring blank-faced into the semidarkness.

After phoning the hospice people to come confirm the time of death, I wandered outside and saw a spectacular haloed moon in the icy sky.

"Oh Burck," Kelli said exultantly, when she came out and saw it too, "you're such a showoff!"

It was the wittiest thing I'd ever heard her say, and this (but not the moon) I attributed to Burck's influence.

MY FATHER HAD TAKEN four days to die, once he'd discovered he could no longer walk to the toilet under his own steam. Meanwhile, back in Oklahoma, my mother was wondering when the hell I'd be coming home. The day before, when it was clear Burck wouldn't be pulling any more rabbits out of his hat, I'd phoned Marlies and said it wouldn't be long now.

"Oh for Christ's sake!" she said. "You can't *do* anything for him. Get back here!"

She was still very much Marlies, though by then her dementia was far enough along that I'd had to remind her whose deathbed I was visiting. Indeed, that was one fortunate aspect of my #MeToo disaster: Had I not been forced to leave my wife and daughter in Virginia, I'm not sure what I would have done about my more-senile-than-we-realized mother. I'd already persuaded her to relinquish her car to my daughter, and later—fourteen months after Burck's death—she would break her hip and have to go, at last, into assisted living.

"When *your* time comes," I told her, while still in Santa Fe, "you'll be glad to have a son who doesn't leave you until you're properly dead."

But now Burck was dead, and I needed to get home and see about Marlies. The next morning (after I'd shared the news with friends and written a cordial note in my Airbnb host's guestbook), I drove to Las Barrancas to say goodbye to my stepfamily—for now anyway, since I still planned to return the following week for Thanksgiving. I felt I owed it to my father, who'd invited me after all, and who might have wanted me to go on normalizing relations with the family he'd left behind. Besides, my Thanksgiving Airbnb was non-refundable by then.

They were all sitting around the kitchen when I arrived, and I got the definite impression they'd left off talking about me. There was an awkward silence while they cast about for some pleasantry, then Aaron asked if I wanted to commune a bit more with my father's body.

"He's still here?" I said, startled.

They nodded. Apparently the Rivera Funeral Home van was still making its rounds elsewhere in that elderly, death-haunted town.

I couldn't resist: "Well, you know what Burck used to say . . ."

"What's that?" said Kelli.

"'When I die, stick a bone up my ass and let the dogs drag me away.'" Silence. I felt obliged to explain: "Whatever's in there"—I pointed toward the back bedroom where my father's sour corpse lay—"it's not Burck."

No titter of recognition at Burck's old saw, perhaps because it was from an earlier era—an earlier Burck: his irreverent younger self, the urbane rationalist who'd won a famous law scholarship and left a hick burg for the big city and made a terrible marriage to my mother. Kelli was looking at me as though I were a boorish job applicant and she a seasoned receptionist who was determined to keep me out of the boss' office.

"Well, you guys," I said, wrapping it up, "better get back to Marlies."

I stood and gave hugs all around. Sandra's came last, and was the most sincere on my part, but it was like squeezing a rag doll.

"See you guys next week!" I called over my shoulder.

They looked at one another. "Wait . . . *what?*" said Kelli.

"For Thanksgiving. Oh, don't worry, I reserved my own Airb—"

"We won't *be* here. I mean—we thought, you know, it'd be best to take Mom away for a while . . ."

I got it. Did I ever. "Of course!" I said—three or four times—and brandished a hand goodbye. I was almost out the door when I was stopped by a need to see, one more time, the only person on the premises who'd loved me and done his imperfect best to keep me somewhere in his life, despite those people in the kitchen. Just a glance from the hallway: the sheets were tucked around his shrinking body, and his face had turned a sort of pearly blue. Somehow they'd managed to close his mouth, or maybe it was just rigor mortis.

ENVOI

"Burck's unfailing spirit of optimism and good will would brighten even the darkest day," the peroration of his obit begins. Neither I nor the younger, more sardonic Burck could have ever written such a line, and I indignantly say as much whenever someone accuses me of having written Burck's obituary. As for the rest of it, well, you'll get no argument from me:

> . . . His intellect, energy, fair-mindedness, thoughtfulness, and exuberant personality were greatly appreciated by his friends and colleagues. Burck was an esteemed teacher and mentor. His was a life well lived.
>
> Burck and Sandra led lives of love and devotion to one another. They loved travel, the out-of-doors, and creatures great and small. Burck is survived by Sandra; sons Blake and Aaron [but not Scott]; daughter, Kelli; and by six grandchildren. He is also survived by his sister, Kay Heiden of McLean, Virginia.

> The family will honor Burck's request that there be
> no service.

I'm sure most of the old friends and colleagues who read that obituary nodded their heads in fond recognition: Burck was indeed a good man who, etc. As for my own obit, the headline—at least in the *Times* (if they bother)—will probably read "Blake Bailey, Writer Accused of Rape, Dies at [age]." And certain people will wonder: How did a good man like Burck sire not one but *two* such rotten sons? I can only tell you that he and I had a lovely rapport for much of our lives, and it never quite went away. We continued to recognize bits of ourselves in each other, even while we became more and more different, at least on the surface.

Certainly I was proud of him and loved him dearly, and certainly he left a hole in my life: My target audience, as a writer, was a man who read only one of my books, and only then because he was in it. And now? Why should I bother to write or do anything, good or bad, when he isn't around to praise or belittle me?—or save me, as he did so many times and was perhaps happiest doing, because he loved me and because it gave him the upper hand.

"Stay strong, be brave, aim high. Tomorrow will be different than today. Time will help."

So every morning I get up and put one foot in front of the other. I read books, exercise regularly, eat with nutrition in mind, try to write a little—because life still *interests* me, oddly enough—and (as Burck/Polonius would have it) grapple friends and family to my soul with hoops of steel. They still love me, and that matters more than the rest of the indifferently roaring world.

Appendix

A FEW THOUGHTS ON W. W. NORTON'S CANCELATION OF *PHILIP ROTH: THE BIOGRAPHY*

"Books must be judged on their content. Many of literature's celebrated authors led troubled— and troubling—lives. The reading public must be allowed to make their own decisions about what to read."

—National Coalition Against Censorship

"Bailey has not been convicted of anything, or even criminally charged, yet the book's publisher,

W. W. Norton, announced it was withdrawing the
book from print. That doesn't make sense and it's a
terrible precedent. . . . Publishers are supposed to
be in the business of expanding access to human
knowledge, art and culture, not extinguishing it.
And if mere accusations of sexual misconduct by an
author are enough to render a book unpublishable,
then the books written by three of our last five
presidents should be unpublished too."
—Kyle Smith, "The Publishing Industry has turned
   into modern-day book burners," *New York Post*

"Bringing out a book should signify that a
publisher believes there is something edifying,
worthwhile or elucidating contained in the volume.
It should not be construed as an endorsement of
the ideas or narrative purveyed, nor of the personal
conduct of the author."
—Suzanne Nossel, PEN America

"[A] major act of censorship, with chilling
implications for democratic rights. . . . Bailey's
book, likely to be the standard work on Roth's life
for some time to come, has been 'pulped' and its
author turned overnight into a 'non-person.' There
is no precedent for this in recent times. . . . Who
is safe from such accusations? Any person can
come forward and accuse a writer, musician, artist
or political figure of 'sex crimes' and the media
will instantly and obediently paint the individual
as an evildoer and help banish the accused from
public life. . . . This is McCarthyism of an especially
pernicious character."
—David Walsh, World Socialist Web Site

"The answer to suppression of expression and ideas isn't greater or responsive suppression, but greater public debate, which is silenced when a publisher prevents readers from reading a book and forming their opinions. A book is larger than its author; it is an addition to the often-contentious public record for posterity."

—Authors Guild

"Are we to be told that we can't read particular books, listen to particular musical works, or look at particular paintings and movies because the creators of those books, musical works, paintings and movies are morally imperfect? According to whose dubious authority? And what, in the end, will we be left with? The Bible and Norman Rockwell? Bear in mind the Bible is very racy in places, and they'll get the goods on Norman Rockwell too, you just wait."

—Blake Bailey, *La Repubblica*

Note: Roughly a month after W. W. Norton's cancelation of Philip Roth: The Biography, *the book was reissued by Skyhorse Publishing in paperback, eBook, and audio editions.*

ABOUT THE AUTHOR

B lake Bailey is the author of biographies of Philip Roth, John Cheever, Richard Yates, and Charles Jackson. He won the National Book Critics Circle Award, the Francis Parkman Prize from the Society of American Historians, a Literature Award from the American Academy of Arts and Letters, and a Guggenheim Fellowship. He was also a finalist for the Pulitzer and James Tait Black Prizes. A previous memoir, *The Splendid Things We Planned*, was a finalist for the National Book Critics Circle Award in Autobiography. He is working on a biography of James Salter.